Take &Read

The Gospel of Luke

Ian Boxall

Edited by Adrian Graffy

Published in 2009 by Alive Publishing Ltd.
Graphic House, 124 City Road, Stoke on Trent, ST4 2PH.
Tel: +44 (0) 1782 745600   Fax: +44 (0) 1782 745500
www.alivepublishing.co.uk

©2009 Alive Publishing
British Library Catalogue-in-Publication Data.
A catalogue record for this book is available from the British Library.

ISBN 978-1-906278-06-9

Contents

Foreword

One of the features of the Church of today is the rediscovery of the Bible. In the years since the Second Vatican Council this thirst for the Scriptures has become stronger and stronger. The desire for a deeper engagement with the Bible is clear from the enormous popularity of publications such as *Walk with Me* and *Bible Alive*.

Take and Read is designed to assist people in their need to understand the Bible more deeply. The series has been developed as a follow-up to the document 'The Gift of Scripture', which was produced in 2005 by the Bishops of England and Wales, and of Scotland, to mark the 40th anniversary of the Council document on Divine Revelation, *Dei Verbum*.

The story of the conversion of Saint Augustine to the Catholic faith inspired the title of the series. He recounts in his 'Confessions' how he heard a voice calling to him with the words *Tolle, lege* 'Take and Read'. At that moment he picked up the New Testament and read the first chapter his eyes fell upon, from the Letter to the Romans. His conversion was assured.

These books are a major new resource for prayerful reading of the Scriptures both for groups and for individuals. Passages from the Gospels are accompanied by commentary, quotations from the Fathers and from Church documents, Christian art and inspiring photographs, as well as suggestions for prayer and reflection.

It is a great pleasure to acknowledge the work of those who helped develop this series. Representatives from dioceses throughout Britain worked on the preparatory stages. Particular thanks should go to Anne White, Anne Dixon and Sister Vicky Hummell. I record my gratitude to the authors who have produced such rich commentary on the gospel passages. I am particularly pleased that Mike and Sue Conway of Alive Publishing agreed to publish the *Take and Read* series.

Take and Read will help you to delve more deeply into the Scriptures, to understand them better, and to pray with the Scriptures. *Take and Read* will assist you in *lectio divina*, that prayerful reading of Scripture which has always been central to the life of the Church.

Fr Adrian Graffy

And behold I heard a voice from a nearby house singing and frequently repeating, like a boy or a girl, I do not know which: Take and read; take and read. I grabbed the book and opened it and I read in silence the first chapter my eyes fell upon.

Augustine Confessions VIII, 29

I pray you, good Jesus,
that as you have graciously granted me to take
in with delight
the words that give knowledge of you,
so you will grant me in your kindness
to come at last to you, the source of all wisdom,
and to stand for ever before your face. Amen.

The Prayer of St Bede (to end a session)

Introduction to the Gospel of Luke

The Gospel of Luke is generally thought to be the third gospel to be written (about 80-85 AD). Mark provides Luke with his basic outline: the baptism and temptation, an account of Jesus' ministry in Galilee, and a journey to Jerusalem culminating in Christ's passion and death and the discovery of the empty tomb. But, like Matthew, Luke makes significant additions to Mark's brief account. Alone among the evangelists, he sets out his reasons for writing in an opening prologue (*Luke* 1:1-4). He prefaces Mark's story with colourful infancy narratives, and ends with memorable resurrection appearances. We are indebted to him for some of the most memorable of Jesus' parables.

Luke is a gifted storyteller, whose stories have had a huge impact on the Christian imagination and Christian art. It is no wonder that Luke became the patron saint of artists. Through his story, we hear the gospel in words and images intelligible to the non-Jewish world, reaching out especially to women and men on the fringes: tax-collectors, prostitutes and sinners; the sick and socially-excluded; Jews, Samaritans and Gentile centurions; the disreputable rich and the dispossessed poor.

Luke also writes like a historian. He locates Jesus' story within both Jewish and Roman history. But his history is not centred on kings, emperors and politicians. Rather it describes how God's Spirit has been at work, in the history of a marginal people (Israel), then in the life of God's rejected Son, and those marginal figures who glimpse salvation in him. Nor does it stop with the gospel. Unlike Matthew, Mark and John, Luke continues into a second volume, the Acts of the Apostles.

This book in the *Take and Read* series comprises twelve sessions, each presenting a section of Luke's gospel for study and prayer. The passages chosen aim to give you a good idea of Luke's story and concerns, and to help you understand his gospel more deeply. However, you will understand Luke better if you read the intervening sections of the gospel in your own Bible.

The Gospel of Luke invites us to embark on a journey of faith and discovery. This journey began when Jesus travelled from Galilee to Jerusalem, and continued in Acts with the journeys of Philip, Peter, Barnabas and Paul. Our own journey of faith is part of this bigger journey, and Luke introduces us to fellow-travellers along the way.

Opposite: The Annunciation of Virgin Mary, Hellenic Art, Greece.

Jesus' Coming Announced

Hear the Word of God

Read Luke 1:26-45

26 In the sixth month the angel Gabriel was sent by God to a town in Galilee called Nazareth, 27 to a virgin engaged to a man whose name was Joseph, of the house of David. The virgin's name was Mary.

28 And he came to her and said, "Greetings, favoured one! The Lord is with you." 29 But she was much perplexed by his words and pondered what sort of greeting this might be.

30 The angel said to her, "Do not be afraid, Mary, for you have found favour with God. 31 And now, you will conceive in your womb and bear a son, and you will name him Jesus. 32 He will be great, and will be called the Son of the Most High, and the Lord God will give to him the throne of his ancestor David. 33 He will reign over the house of Jacob forever, and of his kingdom there will be no end."

34 Mary said to the angel, "How can this be, since I am a virgin?"

35 The angel said to her, "The Holy Spirit will come upon you, and the power of the Most High will overshadow you; therefore the child to be born will be holy; he will be called Son of God. 36 And now, your relative Elizabeth in her old age has also conceived a son; and this is the sixth month for her who was said to be barren. 37 For nothing will be impossible with God."

38 Then Mary said, "Here am I, the servant of the Lord; let it be with me according to your word." Then the angel departed from her.

39 In those days Mary set out and went with haste to a Judean town in the hill country, 40 where she entered the house of Zechariah and greeted Elizabeth.

41 When Elizabeth heard Mary's greeting, the child leaped in her womb. And Elizabeth was filled with the Holy Spirit 42 and exclaimed with a loud cry, "Blessed are you among women, and blessed is the fruit of your womb. 43 And why has this happened to me, that the mother of my Lord comes to me? 44 For as soon as I heard the sound of your greeting, the child in my womb leaped for joy. 45 And blessed is she who believed that there would be a fulfilment of what was spoken to her by the Lord."

Understand the Word of God

This session will explore:

- ❖ the purpose of Luke's infancy narratives
- ❖ the annunciation to Mary
- ❖ the visitation of Mary to Elizabeth
- ❖ the message for today

Setting in the Gospel

Luke's first two chapters (his 'infancy narratives') prepare the ground for Jesus' ministry. He recounts a number of events leading up to the births of John the Baptist and Jesus. Two of these events will be explored in detail in this session. Like a skilled artist, Luke weaves together the destinies of Jesus and John. The births of both are announced by the angel Gabriel; we hear of the circumcision of both according to the Law of Moses.

But Luke also makes clear that John and Jesus are no equals. Jesus is the Lord, the Son of the Most High, whereas John is the prophet who comes to prepare his way. It is important that we get this relationship right before the main story begins.

The Annunciation, c.1438-45 by Fra Angelico, (c.1387-1455).

The annunciation of the coming birth of Samson is found in Judges 13:2-3:

There was a certain man of Zorah, of the tribe of the Danites, whose name was Manoah. His wife was barren, having borne no children. And the angel of the Lord appeared to the woman and said to her, 'Although you are barren, having borne no children, you shall conceive and bear a son.'

What Kind of Text?

The infancy narratives are rather unusual kinds of stories, even within the gospels (and Matthew's and Luke's are quite different from each other). Rich in theological symbolism, they tell us as much about who Jesus is as about what happened to Mary and Joseph in the months surrounding his birth. A particular feature of Luke's narrative is the old-fashioned feel of his Greek, which deliberately imitates the Greek translation of the Old Testament. We are back in the world of ancient Israel: God has now acted in the recent events surrounding Jesus' birth, just as he acted for his people in the ancient past.

Two different kinds of stories are found here. The annunciation to Mary, like that to Zechariah (1:5-23), echoes Old Testament annunciation stories, such as the birth of Samson in Judges 13:2-7. Such stories announced births of particularly significant figures, often despite impediments like barrenness or old age. But, unlike the Old Testament annunciations, and that to Zechariah, the announcement here is unique. The angel Gabriel foretells a virginal conception.

The visitation story brings together for the first time the two sets of relatives: John's mother Elizabeth, and Jesus' mother Mary. Although regularly painted by artists, this scene is more of a dialogue than one of action. Mary comes in haste, and eventually departs, echoing Luke's theme of the journey. But the focus is on the exchange of words between the two women.

The Visitation by Bartholomaeus Bruyn (1493-1555)

Commentary: verse by verse reading

The Annunciation to Mary

vv.26-27 The annunciation takes place 'in the sixth month' of the pregnancy of Elizabeth, reported in Luke 1:24. The archangel Gabriel, who has already announced John's birth, now comes to Jesus' mother. Gabriel is one of the seven archangels who 'stand in the presence of God' (*Luke* 1:19). Luke pays great attention to such appearances by angelic messengers. No less than the temple in Jerusalem where Gabriel appears to Zechariah (*Luke* 1:11), Mary's ordinary house becomes a holy place where heaven and earth meet.

Mary's hometown of Nazareth is unknown in the Old Testament. It is appropriate that the Christ who comes for the marginalised is brought up in an obscure Galilean village. Yet he is also born into royal circles: his mother is betrothed to Joseph, of the royal line of David. Jewish marriage was a two-stage affair: the first stage has taken place, but Joseph has not taken Mary into his family home. Mary is described here as a 'virgin' (Greek *parthenos*), evoking the prophecy of Isaiah 7:14 which Matthew explicitly cites (*Matthew* 1:23).

vv.28-29 The greeting of Gabriel, in the Latin Vulgate translation, gives us the opening words of the Hail Mary: 'Hail, full of grace'. Luke's Greek is better translated 'Greetings, favoured one' or 'Hail, gifted one'. The emphasis is on God's gracious action towards Mary, choosing her as the mother of his Son. The statement that 'the Lord is with you' echoes Old Testament claims for Jerusalem: the Lord is in the midst of her, as his holy city.

vv.30-34 The heart of Gabriel's announcement is the miraculous conception of Jesus, despite Mary being a virgin. The literal translation of verse 34 is 'since I do not know a man'. Fear is the appropriate response to the awesomeness of God, and regularly experienced by those who encounter his angels. But Mary need not fear, because she is the recipient of good news.

Tobit 12:14-15 another angel presents himself.

'I was sent to you to test you. And at the same time God sent me to heal you and Sarah your daughter-in-law. I am Raphael, one of the seven angels who stand ready and enter before the glory of the Lord.'

Matthew 1:22-23:

All this took place to fulfil what had been spoken by the Lord through the prophet: 'Look, the virgin shall conceive and bear a son, and they shall name him Emmanuel,' which means, 'God is with us.'

'Sing aloud, O daughter Zion;
shout, O Israel! ...
The king of Israel, the Lord, is in your midst;
You shall fear disaster no more.'
(Zephaniah 3:14-15)

The description of Jesus as the Son who will inherit David's throne forever picks up Nathan's prophecy to King David centuries before in 2 Samuel 7:12-14. After several centuries without a Davidic king, God's promises to his people are finally being fulfilled in Jesus.

vv.35-37 Despite superficial similarities, the conception of Jesus is very different from pagan stories of gods fathering children by human mothers. What Luke describes is not a god impregnating a woman, but a new act of God's creative power.

The Spirit which hovered over the waters at creation (*Genesis* 1) is now active in the conception of God's Son. The God who 'overshadowed' Moses and the people in the wilderness (*Exodus* 40:35) now overshadows his servant Mary with his saving presence.

There are echoes too of the story of Abraham and Sarah: in the reference to the old and barren Elizabeth as a sign confirming Gabriel's words (*Genesis* 17:17), and in the angel's statement that 'nothing will be impossible with God' (*Genesis* 18:14). The wonderful birth of Isaac to Sarah brought into existence the people of Israel. The births of John and Jesus will inaugurate a new people, who will call Abraham their father in faith.

v.38 Yet Mary is no passive recipient of God's gift. Her free yes to God and active participation in God's plan is crucial for it to come into effect. Moreover, Luke's positive portrayal of Mary is not primarily because she is to be Christ's mother. Rather, it is because she is the first of her Son's disciples, accepting God's word, pondering it and allowing it to work in her life. Luke 2:19 reads: 'But Mary treasured all these words and pondered them in her heart.' Luke presents Mary as a prime example of Jesus' words: 'My mother and my brothers are those who hear the word of God and do it.' (*Luke* 8:21)

The Visitation

vv.39-40 It is quite a journey for a pregnant woman to walk from Galilee in the north to the hill-country of Judea in the south (over a hundred miles). Mary's haste to reach her cousin Elizabeth echoes her keen response to God's call. It also picks up on a theme running throughout Luke's gospel and into Acts: responding to God means embarking on a journey and the destination may not always be clear. To begin the journey requires a great leap of faith.

v.41a This leap of faith is met with a leap of joy: that of John the Baptist in Elizabeth's womb when the two women meet. In the Old Testament, leaping is how one welcomes God's coming (*Psalm* 113:4,6 *Malachi* 4:2), and one of Luke's favourite words for describing reaction to Christ's coming is joy.

Some texts in which Luke speaks of the joy of welcoming Christ:

2:10 The angel said to the shepherds: 'Do not be afraid; for see – I am bringing you good news of great joy for all the people: to you is born this day in the city of David a Saviour, who is the Messiah, the Lord.'

15:7 Just so, I tell you, there will be more joy in heaven over one sinner who repents than over ninety-nine righteous persons who need no repentance.

10:17 The seventy returned with joy, saying, 'Lord, in your name even the demons submit to us!'

24:52 They worshipped him, and returned to Jerusalem with great joy.

Judean wilderness

Unlike the 'leaping' or 'stirring' of Esau and Jacob in Rebekah's womb (*Genesis* 25:22), which anticipated their later rivalry, John's leaping acknowledges Jesus' supremacy. Jesus is the Lord, John his herald. Even before his birth, before he can speak words or articulate thoughts, the unborn John responds joyfully to the coming of Christ.

vv.41b-45 When Luke tells us that Elizabeth was 'filled with the Holy Spirit', he is painting her in the role of a prophet. God chooses the most unlikely people, such as this elderly woman, to proclaim what he is doing in human lives. She certainly speaks with incredible prophetic insight, not only about her own unborn child but also about Mary's child.

In this powerful scene, we see two women of incredible faith, who trust in God and open themselves up to his Spirit despite immense difficulties. Elizabeth has spent a long life without children, which in her world would have been a cause of shame as well as immense sorrow. Mary's shame is just beginning: that of a young woman, probably hardly a teenager, who falls pregnant before her marriage to Joseph is completed. In the light of this, the joy expressed by both women is amazing.

Within the Lucan narrative, two particular scenes invite reflection on the place of Mary in the life of the Church: the Annunciation and the visit to Elizabeth. These passages emphasise that Mary is in a unique way the recipient of God's election and grace.

(Anglican-Roman Catholic International Commission, Mary: Grace and Hope in Christ n. 15)

The Visitation by Jesus Mafa

The Word Lives On

These two stories are only found in Luke's Gospel. Matthew recounts an angelic annunciation to Joseph, in which some of the same themes occur: a virginal conception, a call to name the child Jesus, the importance of Jesus' Davidic ancestry (*Matthew* 1:18-25).

Both scenes continue to play an important role in Christian devotion. They each contribute phrases to the Hail Mary. They also provide two of the five Joyful Mysteries of the Rosary. Luke's Visitation account introduces Mary's canticle, the *Magnificat* (1:46-55), sung or recited at Evening Prayer. The two scenes have also been particular favourites of artists, among them Fra Angelico, El Greco and Rogier van der Weyden.

In the Lectionary

The Annunciation (1:26-38) is read on the 4th Sunday of Advent in Year B, and the Visitation (1:39-45) on the same Sunday in Year C. They are also set for 20th and 21st December in the Weekday Lectionary.

Not surprisingly, verses 26-38 are set for the Feast of the Annunciation, and vv. 39-56 (including the *Magnificat*) for the Visitation. The Annunciation also provides the gospel for the Feast of the Immaculate Conception, and the Visitation provides the gospel for the Assumption.

Hail, Mary, full of grace! The Lord is with you! (words of the angel Gabriel in Luke 1:28)

Blessed art thou among women and blessed is the fruit of thy womb, Jesus! (words of Elizabeth in Luke 1:42)

The Visitation by Rogier van der Weyden, Galleria Sabauda, Turin, Italy.

La visitation :
Marie rend visite
a Elisabeth. from
School of Troyes

Live the Word of God

Listen again to the reading: Luke 1:26-45

What do you hear now?

Suggestions for reflection and prayer

What are the differences between Mary's response to the angel, and that of Zechariah (Luke 1:11-22)?

Reflect on the mutual sharing of joy between Mary and Elizabeth at the Visitation, and what this might teach us about evangelisation.

Reflect on the words of St Ambrose on this page.

Mary is promised that her Son's kingdom will have no end.

❖ Pray to be open to the breaking in of God's kingdom in our lives.

Mary is promised that the Holy Spirit will overshadow her.

❖ Pray that the Holy Spirit may overshadow and transform our lives.

Elizabeth blesses Mary for trusting that God's word will be fulfilled.

❖ Pray for the grace to study and understand God's word more deeply.

Ambrose, Bishop of Milan (c. 339-397), wrote these words about the Visitation:

You see that Mary did not doubt but believed and therefore obtained the fruit of faith. 'Blessed … are you who have believed.' But you also are blessed who have heard and believed. For a soul that has believed has both conceived and bears the Word of God and declares his works. Let the soul of Mary be in each of you, so that it magnifies the Lord. Let the spirit of Mary be in each of you, so that it rejoices in God.

(Exposition of the Gospel of Luke 2.26)

A Surprising Birth

Hear the Word of God

Read Luke 2:1-20

[1] In those days a decree went out from Emperor Augustus that all the world should be registered. [2] This was the first registration and was taken while Quirinius was governor of Syria.

[3] All went to their own towns to be registered. [4] Joseph also went from the town of Nazareth in Galilee to Judea, to the city of David called Bethlehem, because he was descended from the house and family of David. [5] He went to be registered with Mary, to whom he was engaged and who was expecting a child.

[6] While they were there, the time came for her to deliver her child. [7] And she gave birth to her firstborn son and wrapped him in bands of cloth, and laid him in a manger, because there was no place for them in the inn.

[8] In that region there were shepherds living in the fields, keeping watch over their flock by night. [9] Then an angel of the Lord stood before them, and the glory of the Lord shone around them, and they were terrified. [10] But the angel said to them, 'Do not be afraid; for see — I am bringing you good news of great joy for all the people: [11] to you is born this day in the city of David a Saviour, who is the Messiah, the Lord. [12] This will be a sign for you: you will find a child wrapped in bands of cloth and lying in a manger.'

[13] And suddenly there was with the angel a multitude of the heavenly host, praising God and saying, [14] 'Glory to God in the highest heaven, and on earth peace among those whom he favours!'

[15] When the angels had left them and gone into heaven, the shepherds said to one another, 'Let us go now to Bethlehem and see this thing that has taken place, which the Lord has made known to us.' [16] So they went with haste and found Mary and Joseph, and the child lying in the manger.

[17] When they saw this, they made known what had been told them about this child; [18] and all who heard it were amazed at what the shepherds told them. [19] But Mary treasured all these words and pondered them in her heart. [20] The shepherds returned, glorifying and praising God for all they had heard and seen, as it had been told them.

Opposite:The Nativity, c.1305, Giotto di Bondone, Scrovegni (Arena) Chapel, Padua, Italy.

Understand the Word of God

- ❖ the purpose of the birth narrative
- ❖ the annunciation to the shepherds
- ❖ how these stories anticipate the rest of Luke's Gospel
- ❖ the message for today

Setting in the Gospel

Following the story of John the Baptist's birth, naming and circumcision, Luke recounts another birth, that of Jesus. We have been left with a brief description in Luke 1:80 of John growing up, maturing in the Spirit, and biding his time in the wilderness, where we will meet him next at Luke 3:1-2. Now the scene is set for the arrival of the one whose forerunner John is.

Typical of Luke is his concern to locate this world-changing birth in history. Hence we learn that Augustus (27 BC – 14 AD) is on the imperial throne, and the world is literally on the move as a result of his imperial decree. The holy family are not the only travellers at the time of this momentous event.

The journey of Mary, Joseph and the child will continue to the holy city of Jerusalem, where Jesus will be presented in the temple (*Luke* 2:22-40) in accordance with the law of Moses. Like the later apocryphal gospels, Luke is also interested in the 'hidden years' of Jesus' life. Hence the holy family will travel to Jerusalem once more before Jesus' public ministry begins. As a twelve year old Jesus is taken there on pilgrimage, where he is discovered in the temple, astounding the teachers (*Luke* 2:41-51).

The document on the Bible of the Bishops of England and Wales, and of Scotland, The Gift of Scripture, has this to say about the apocryphal gospels:

Later 'apocryphal' gospels, many of which have been studied by scholars in recent times, were not added to the Christian canon, for they frequently give exaggerated accounts, and portrayals of Jesus and his teaching which are difficult to reconcile with those found in the four canonical gospels.

(paragraph 44)

What Kind of Text?

The ancient world was familiar with birth stories associating the birth of a great figure with extraordinary events. Thus Luke's account would appeal to Gentiles as well as Jews. As Christmas cribs remind us, it weaves together the mundane with the heavenly. An apparently unremarkable birth is shown to be remarkable by its connection with the emperor's political concerns and the appearance of choirs of angels.

The latter feature means that this is not simply a birth story. It also contains an annunciation story, with similar elements to the annunciations to Zechariah and Mary: the appearance of an angel of the Lord, a command not to be afraid, and the promise of a sign.

For ease of study, the passage breaks neatly into four sections: the census (verses 1-5), the birth of Jesus (verses 6-7), the annunciation to the shepherds (verses 8-14) and the visit of the shepherds and their response (verses 15-20).

Statue of Caesar Augustus at the Vatican.

Commentary: verse by verse reading

The Emperor's Census

vv.1-2 In mentioning Augustus' census, Luke is keen to show that the birth of Jesus has an impact even on the empire of Rome. In his eagerness to do so, however, he almost certainly makes a chronological error. The census under Quirinius – which was a local rather than empire-wide census – should be dated to 6 AD. Luke and Matthew, however, agree in locating the events surrounding Jesus' conception and birth to the reign of Herod the Great, who died in 4 BC (*Matthew* 2:1 and *Luke* 1:5).

Micah 5:2 But you, O Bethlehem of Ephrathah, who are one of the little clans of Judah, from you shall come forth for me one who is to rule in Israel.

Matthew 2:1 In the time of King Herod, after Jesus was born in Bethlehem of Judea, wise men from the East came to Jerusalem.

vv.3-5 As with his account of the visitation, Luke again stresses the theme of journeying. The prophecy of Micah 5:2 expected the Messiah's birth to take place in Bethlehem, the birthplace of King David (1 *Samuel* 16). Luke agrees with Matthew 2:1 on this point and typically describes the small town Bethlehem as 'the city of David', a title normally given to David's more impressive capital of Jerusalem, some six miles to the north. Just like backwater Nazareth, the 'little town of Bethlehem' plays a central role in God's plan to save those on the margins.

Church of the Nativity, Bethlehem. View from the Armenian Transept towards the Nave.

The Birth of Jesus

v.6 Like the parallel account in Matthew (*Matthew* 2:1), Luke's account of Jesus' birth is surprisingly brief. Nevertheless, it is full of meaning. When Luke tells us that 'the time came for her to deliver her child', for example, he is not simply referring to the end of Mary's nine months of pregnancy. Rather, Christ enters our world when God's time is right. As St Paul puts it, writing to the Galatians: 'But when the fulness of time had come, God sent his Son, born of a woman, born under the law.' (*Galatians* 4:4).

v.7 Yet although God's time is right, humanity is not ready to receive God's Son. Luke points out the irony that the child born to inherit David's throne has such a poor reception in David's town. There is no room for him in the ***kataluma***: though generally translated as 'inn', this Greek word could mean 'guest room', perhaps in a relative's house. The same word is used of the 'guest room' in Luke 22:11, which the disciples prepared for Jesus to eat the Passover. The manger would then be located in the area of the house where the animals slept.

Some have detected in the wrapping of the baby in bands of cloth and laying him in the manger an echo of the end of the story. After his crucifixion, Jesus is wrapped in a linen cloth and laid in a tomb (*Luke* 23:53). The one who is born for us is also the one who will die for us.

The Venerable Bede (c. 673-735) writes of the appropriate timing of Christ's birth:

In the forty-second year of Caesar Augustus, twenty-seven years from the death of Cleopatra and Antony when Egypt became a province, the third year after the 193rd Olympiad, 752 years from the foundation of the city, that is in that year whence by the ordaining of God Caesar imposed a most sure and true peace, Jesus Christ the son of God consecrated the sixth age of the world by his coming.

(Bede, The Reckoning of Time)

Luke's reference to a 'manger', a trough for animal feed, and the following verse from the Book of Isaiah seem to have led to the inclusion of animals in the crib scene.

The ox knows it owner,
and the donkey its master's crib,
but Israel does not know,
my people do not understand.
(Isaiah 1:3)

The New Born Child, late 1640s, Georges de la Tour, Musee des Beaux-Arts, Rennes, France.

The Annunciation to the Shepherds

v.8 Shepherds were among the poorest of Jewish society, who lived much of the time on the fringes, 'in the fields' outside of town. Luke's concentration on the shepherds' role in the story is in marked contrast to Matthew's magi, with their expensive gifts. He highlights how the Saviour reaches out in a special way to the poor and marginal among his people.

v.9 Like the humble country priest Zechariah, and Mary of Nazareth, these shepherds appear unlikely candidates for an angelic visitation. But perhaps we are meant to remember that the great King David started life as a humble shepherd-boy in Bethlehem. This makes these shepherds highly appropriate recipients of the good news that a descendant of David, a new shepherd-king, has been born.

The Priene Inscription, found in Asia Minor, describes the birth of the 'Saviour' Emperor Augustus in these terms:
The birthday of the god heralded the beginning of good news for the whole world.

vv.10-11 The angel's message challenges our human perceptions of power. The language used echoes that normally applied in the Roman world to the emperor and the empire. The Emperor Augustus was often acclaimed as 'Saviour' for bringing peace to the Mediterranean. 'Good news' or 'gospel' was used to describe imperial proclamations. The subversive heavenly message is that true power, and the gift of true peace, is to be found in this tiny, vulnerable baby, born in a backwater of the great empire.

Three titles are given to Jesus here. As well as its imperial associations for non-Jews, the title 'Saviour' is used in the Old Testament for God, who saves his people. 'Messiah' or 'anointed one' describes a figure anointed by God to act on his behalf in the last days. The context suggests that Luke is thinking of a royal Messiah, the anointed king of David's line. Finally, the child will be 'the Lord', a word used in the Greek translation of the Old Testament of God himself.

Luke 5:11 When they had brought their boats to shore, they left everything and followed him.
Luke 5:28 And Levi got up, left everything, and followed him.

v.12 Like Zechariah and Mary, the shepherds are given a sign, confirming the angel's message. But in order to see the sign, they have to leave their workplace and embark on a journey. Later on in Luke's gospel, disciples of Jesus will have to do exactly the same.

vv.13-14 The angel is now joined by heavenly choirs: 'the heavenly host' means the heavenly army, which is more than a match for the armies of the Roman emperor. Their song provides the third canticle so far in Luke's infancy narrative.

A similar song will be sung by the crowds during Jesus' triumphal entry into Jerusalem at Luke 19:38. The ancient manuscripts have two different readings of the angels' words. Our translation ('on earth peace among those whom he favours') is probably preferable to the alternative: 'on earth peace, good will among people'. The emphasis is upon God's good will or favour, which is the source of true peace.

The canticles in Luke's Infancy Narratives:

Luke 1:46-55 Mary's Magnificat, her song of thanksgiving

Luke 1:68-79 Zechariah's Benedictus at the birth of John

Luke 2:14 The Gloria of the angels, sung at Christ's birth

Luke 2:29-32

The Annunciation to the Shepherds by Benjamin Gerritsz Cuyp, Hermitage, St. Petersburg, Russia.

The Visit of the Shepherds

vv.15-16 Having heard the angelic announcement, the shepherds now go to see the sign which confirms that message: the fragile baby lying in a manger. 'This thing that has taken place' could also mean 'this word which has come to pass'. The shepherds have received God's word from an angel, and now must witness to this word.

vv.17-18 Now the shepherds must become evangelists, spreading the good news or 'gospel' of peace they have received. So they do what preachers of the gospel are to do: they make known what they have been told about this child, and what he has come to do.

v.19 Again, we meet Mary the faithful disciple, who treasures all these 'things' or 'words', and ponders them in her heart. The good news of the incarnation is not something that can be rushed, or understood quickly, or proclaimed superficially. It needs to be meditated upon, discussed, pondered in the depths of our hearts.

v.20 Finally, the shepherds return to their former lives, changed by their experience. Their overwhelming experience of encountering the Christ child leads them to glorify and praise God. Later, during Luke's account of Jesus' ministry, this will be the reaction of those who see what God is doing in his healings.

Luke 5:26 (at the healing of the paralytic) Amazement seized all of them, and they glorified God and were filled with awe, saying, 'We have seen strange things today.'

Luke 7:16 (after the raising to life of the widow's son at Nain) Fear seized all of them; and they glorified God, saying, 'A great prophet has risen among us!' and 'God has looked favourably on his people!'

The Word Lives On

The story of Jesus' birth is found only in two gospels, Luke's and Matthew's. As already noted, Matthew's account is quite different from Luke's, focusing on the magi as representatives of the Gentile world. Matthew also suggests that Bethlehem, rather than Nazareth, was the hometown of Mary and Joseph.

Both stories, and particularly Luke's, have influenced the Christian imagination regarding Christ's Nativity. Artistic portrayals generally focus on the child in the manger. St Francis was particularly inspired by Luke's scene when he established the first crib at Greccio. Liturgically, the song of the heavenly host has provided the opening words for the Gloria.

The Adoration of the Shepherds by Andrea Mantegna, 1450.

In the Lectionary

The first part of Luke's nativity story (2:1-14) provides the gospel for Christmas Midnight Mass, and the story continues (2:15-20) at the Dawn Mass. Luke 2:16-21 is set for the Solemnity of Mary, Mother of God (1st January).

Statue of the Blessed Virgin Mary and Christ, St. James Cathedral, Seattle. Photograph by Michael Ziegler.

Live the Word of God

Listen again to the reading: Luke 1:26-45

What do you hear now?
Suggestions for reflection and prayer.

What aspects of the story stand out for you? Why might this be?

What can we learn from God's choice of the shepherds to witness the birth of Christ? What might this have to teach today's Church?

Mary 'treasured all these things and pondered them in her heart'. Reflect on the mystery of God becoming one of us, and what it means for our lives.

Mary and Joseph seek shelter in Bethlehem as they wait for the birth of Jesus.
❖ Pray for those awaiting the safe delivery of their child.

The shepherds are promised the sign of a baby lying in a manger.
❖ Pray for the grace to see God's presence among us, especially in the weak and vulnerable.

The shepherds make known what they have seen and heard, and praise God.
❖ Pray for the wisdom and courage to share our faith, through our words and our actions.

Preach the Gospel at all times, and when necessary use words (St Francis of Assisi).

Rejection in Nazareth

Hear the Word of God

Read Luke 4:16-30

[16] When he came to Nazareth, where he had been brought up, he went to the synagogue on the sabbath day, as was his custom. He stood up to read, [17] and the scroll of the prophet Isaiah was given to him. He unrolled the scroll and found the place where it was written:

[18] 'The Spirit of the Lord is upon me, because he has anointed me to bring good news to the poor. He has sent me to proclaim release to the captives and recovery of sight to the blind, to let the oppressed go free, [19] to proclaim the year of the Lord's favour.'

[20] And he rolled up the scroll, gave it back to the attendant, and sat down. The eyes of all in the synagogue were fixed on him. [21] Then he began to say to them, 'Today this scripture has been fulfilled in your hearing.'

[22] All spoke well of him and were amazed at the gracious words that came from his mouth. They said, 'Is not this Joseph's son?' [23] He said to them, 'Doubtless you will quote to me this proverb, 'Doctor, cure yourself!' And you will say, 'Do here also in your hometown the things that we have heard you did at Capernaum.'

[24] And he said, 'Truly I tell you, no prophet is accepted in the prophet's hometown. [25] But the truth is, there were many widows in Israel in the time of Elijah, when the heaven was shut up three years and six months, and there was a severe famine over all the land; [26] yet Elijah was sent to none of them except to a widow at Zarephath in Sidon. [27] There were also many lepers in Israel in the time of the prophet Elisha, and none of them was cleansed except Naaman the Syrian.'

[28] When they heard this, all in the synagogue were filled with rage. [29] They got up, drove him out of the town, and led him to the brow of the hill on which their town was built, so that they might hurl him off the cliff. [30] But he passed through the midst of them and went on his way.

Opposite: Jesus teaching in the Synagogue, c. 1897 (from 'Life of Our Saviour Jesus Christ' by J.J. Tissot)

Understand the Word of God

This session will explore:

- ❖ Luke's Nazareth episode, and those in the other gospels
- ❖ its place within Luke's story
- ❖ Jesus' role as Prophet-Messiah
- ❖ the message for today

Setting in the Gospel

Luke has just introduced us to the adult Jesus, who begins his work at about the age of thirty (3:23). Though Jesus is certainly the Jewish Messiah, Luke's version of his genealogy does not simply link him to David and Abraham, as in Matthew chapter 1. Rather, he has come as the representative and Saviour of all humanity, the son of Adam (3:38).

He has received the Spirit at his baptism, and been led by the Spirit into the wilderness. So now it is in the power of the Spirit that Jesus returns to Galilee to begin his public ministry (*Luke* 4:14).

This episode at Nazareth is placed by Luke at the very beginning of Jesus' public ministry. Matthew and Mark, by contrast, describe Jesus' rejection at Nazareth at a later stage (*Matthew* 13:53-58 *Mark* 6:1-6), and without much of Luke's detail. For Luke, this event in Nazareth's synagogue is vital for understanding the rest of Christ's ministry. As the anointed Messiah, he will bring good news to the poor and proclaim the year of the Lord's favour. But he will also be rejected, even by those closest to him.

What Kind of Text?

The version of the story in Matthew and Mark is a conflict story, one of those stories in which opposition to Jesus, or to his followers, is expressed by particular groups, such as the scribes, the Pharisees, or the townspeople. Such conflicts may tell us as much about later tensions between the church and the synagogue as about the difficulties encountered during Jesus' ministry.

Luke's expansion of the story in Matthew and Mark has made it into something quite different. It has become an inauguration story for Jesus' ministry, in which Jesus speaks and acts like one of Israel's prophets. He reads from the great prophet Isaiah. He compares his own ministry to that of the Old Testament prophets Elijah and Elisha. He speaks prophetic words of challenge as well as comfort. Hearing this story, we are to think of Jesus as the anointed prophet as well as the anointed king.

Much of this passage comprises a speech of Jesus, which is another familiar feature of Luke. In Acts in particular, important characters will deliver speeches at crucial points in the narrative, such as Peter's speech at Pentecost. Following ancient convention, these speeches are probably Luke's own creations. They are important for understanding the surrounding story, offering a theological commentary on the action. Hence we should pay particular attention to the words of Jesus' homily here.

Commentary: verse by verse reading

Jesus reads from Isaiah

Luke 2:40 The child grew and became strong, filled with wisdom; and the favour of God was upon him.

Luke 2:52 And Jesus increased in wisdom and in years, and in divine and human favour.

v.16 Jesus returns to the place of his upbringing, Nazareth in Galilee. Luke calls it by its ancient Semitic name Nazara. Luke places more stress than other evangelists upon Jesus' upbringing and the human influences upon him. He is keen to show us that Jesus, like his relation John the Baptist, must grow up, learn and mature. God's Son is truly human, with a human family, and undergoes a human education.

This human education extends to a particular culture and religious tradition. Christ comes among us at a specific time and in a specific place. He inhabits the world of first century Palestinian Judaism. Like other observant male Jews, he regularly attends synagogue on the sabbath.

The origins of the Jewish synagogue are shrouded in mystery. It was originally probably a meeting place and house of study. By the first century synagogues seem to have played an important role also as places of prayer, alongside the Jerusalem temple which was the place for offering sacrifice.

Our Saviour Subject to his Parents at Nazareth, 1860 John Herbert, (1810-90)

The Great Isaiah Scroll from Qumran.

vv.17-19 These verses are important for the light they shed on the synagogue liturgy, though they may reflect the synagogue worship of Luke's own day rather than the practice in Jesus' time. This seems to have included readings from scripture – which would have begun with a reading from the Torah or Pentateuch, followed by a reading from the prophets, as here – and a homily or sermon. When Jesus stands up in the Nazareth synagogue, he reads from the beginning of Isaiah chapter 61. The text of Isaiah that Luke follows contains some variation from the original. It has no reference to binding up the broken-hearted (*Isaiah* 61:1).

The theme of Isaiah's prophecy echoes key themes which are important to Luke: the offer of salvation to the poor, the marginalised, and those in dire circumstances. As Luke's account of the ministry unfolds, we shall see Jesus fulfilling Isaiah's prophecy stage by stage. He will give sight to the blind, and liberate those oppressed by sickness and social exclusion. In his Beatitudes in Luke 6:20-26 he will proclaim good news to the poor.

The original text in the Book of Isaiah reads:

The spirit of the Lord God is upon me,
because the Lord has anointed me;
he has sent me to bring good news to the oppressed,
to bind up the broken-hearted,
to proclaim liberty to the captives,
and release to the prisoners;
to proclaim the year of the Lord's favour,
and the day of vengeance of our God;
to comfort all who mourn.
(Isaiah 61:1-2)

The great Alexandrian biblical scholar Origen (about 185-254) writes this about the scene in the synagogue:

When Jesus had read this passage, he rolled up 'the scroll, gave it to the servant, and sat down. And the eyes of all in the synagogue were fixed on him'. Now too, if you want it, your eyes can be fixed on the Saviour in this synagogue, here in this assembly. When you direct the principal power of seeing in your heart to wisdom and truth and to contemplating God's Only-Begotten, your eyes gaze on Jesus.

(Homilies on the Gospel of Luke 32.6)

A favourable Reaction

v.20 Having read from the prophets, Jesus hands the scroll back to the synagogue attendant, probably for it to be replaced in the sacred ark where the biblical scrolls were kept. He sits down in order to deliver his sermon. Sitting rather than standing is the appropriate position for teaching. Here we reach the turning-point in the story. Luke creates dramatic literary tension by describing the attentiveness of the congregation: 'The eyes of all in the synagogue were fixed on him'.

Interior of the Ancient Synagogue at Nazareth.

v.21 Despite being sometimes viewed as the 'gospel for the Gentiles', Luke's gospel reveals a strong concern to show how Jesus fulfils the Old Testament scriptures. It is important to be able to show that the good news is not something radically new, or for Gentiles only, but part of God's intended plan for Israel as set out in the prophets. At the root of this is a theological concern. God has not changed his mind, but is utterly consistent and to be trusted. What he promised to do he has now done.

v.22 The initial reaction of Jesus' townspeople is favourable. He is the local boy made good, their home-grown prophet. They think of him as the son of Joseph. But the reader of the gospel, in the light of the infancy narrative, knows the bigger picture. He is only 'thought' to be Joseph's son (*Luke* 3:23). As Gabriel has announced, he is 'Son of the Most High' (*Luke* 1:32).

Basilica of the Annunciation at Nazareth.

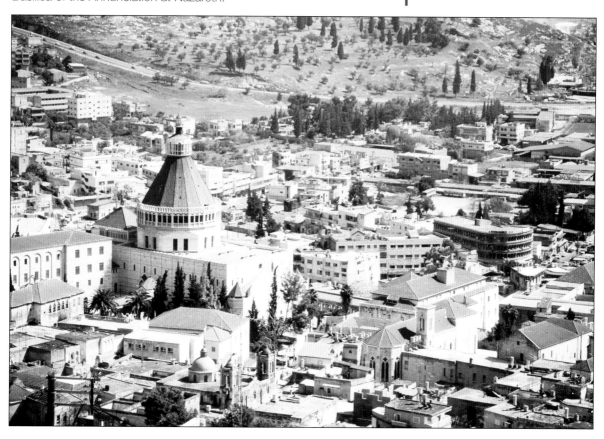

Capernaum (probably meaning 'village of Nahum') is a fishing village about twenty miles away from Nazareth on the north-western shore of the Sea of Galilee, which becomes the focus of Jesus' public ministry. Matthew 4:13 reads: 'He left Nazareth and made his home in Capernaum by the sea, in the territory of Zebulun and Naphtali.'

The Hellenistic orator and philosopher Dio Chrysostom, who was born about 40 AD, gives this version of the proverb:

For all philosophers life is hard in their own country.

v.23 Jesus' first words seem out of place given the favourable response of the people of Nazareth. He cites a well-known proverb about a doctor healing himself, as if to provoke hostility and opposition despite their initial positive reaction. Variant forms of this saying about a physician can be found in both Jewish and Greek writings of the time.

Moreover, the expectation that Jesus will do in Nazareth the things he did in Capernaum – probably miracles – is out of place in Luke's chronological rearrangement, for he does not go to Capernaum until verse 31.

v.24 Another proverb places him firmly in the role of the prophet. Variants of this saying are found in Matthew 13:57, Mark 6:4 and John 4:44, as well as in the apocryphal Gospel of Thomas. It highlights the lonely vocation of prophets, who are regularly rejected by those closest to them.

vv.25-26 As Jesus' sermon continues, we gain a clearer picture of what kind of prophet he will be. The people of Nazareth want him as their prophet, perhaps one they can keep under their control. But Jesus' mission is far wider, extending beyond Israel's boundaries to include the Gentile world. To illustrate this, he models himself on two characters from Israel's past. The first is the prophet Elijah. The miracles he worked for a non-Jewish widow in Zarephath are described at 1 Kings 17.

vv.27 Similarly, Elijah's disciple Elisha is also remembered as an Israelite prophet whose ministry extended to the non-Jewish world. In 2 Kings 5 we hear how Elisha cures Naaman the Syrian of leprosy. Both Elisha and Elijah anticipate what Jesus comes to do.

However, though Jesus prepares the way for this wider prophetic mission, Luke does not describe any direct encounter between Jesus and Gentiles during his public ministry. He omits the story of the Syro-Phoenician woman (*Mark* 7:24-30 *Matthew* 15:21-28), and reworks the story of the centurion's servant so that the centurion does not actually meet Jesus (7:1-10; compare *Matthew* 8:5-13). It will be left to the post-Easter Church in the Acts of the Apostles to preach the gospel to Gentiles.

v.28 Jesus' appeal to Elijah and Elisha leads to the dramatic change from positive to negative reaction. Jesus' fellow Nazarenes realise that they cannot claim him as their own prophet. They object to the idea that the anointed one has come not simply for them, but for outsiders too.

vv. 28-30 The story ends with a cliff-hanger, literally and metaphorically. Jesus is driven to the brow of the hill on which Nazareth stands, in danger of being thrown off the cliff. The theme of the prophet's rejection comes to the fore. But the episode ends with another kind of cliff-hanger: will this divided reaction to Jesus from his own people continue in the remainder of the story? How will we react to this Christ who often challenges and disturbs us?

Compare the texts of the story of the centurion's servant in Luke and Matthew:

Luke 7:3 When the centurion heard about Jesus, he sent some Jewish elders to him, asking him to come and heal his slave.

Matthew 8:5-6 A centurion came to him, appealing to him and saying, 'Lord, my servant is lying at home paralysed, in terrible distress.'

Verse 30 reads: He passed through the midst of them and went on his way. A similar escape of Jesus is reported in John 8:59: They picked up stones to throw at him, but Jesus hid himself and went out of the temple.

Print Depicting Elijah carried to Heaven in a fiery chariot while watched by Elisha.

The Word Lives on

This episode, in a shorter version, has already been used by Mark and Matthew. Luke's focus on Jesus fulfilling the scriptures develops a motif which will become increasingly important for the Fathers of the Church. Whatever the prophet understood by his original words, this passage from Isaiah finds a deeper fulfilment in the ministry of Jesus.

In the Lectionary

Combined with Luke's Prologue, the beginning of this episode provides the gospel for the Third Sunday in Ordinary Time in Year C (Luke 1:1-4 and 4:14-21). The second part (Luke 4:21-30) is set for the following Sunday.

In the Weekday Lectionary, Luke 4:14-22 is set for the 10th January, and 4:24-30 for Monday in the Third Week of Lent. Luke 4:16-21 is set as the gospel for the Mass of Chrism on Maundy Thursday. The whole passage is read on Monday of the twenty-second week in Ordinary Time.

Synagogue scroll.

Live the Word of God

Listen again to the reading: Luke 4:16-30

What do you hear now?
Suggestions for reflection and prayer

How do you think you would have reacted to Jesus' sermon in Nazareth?

What does it mean for Christ to fulfil the Old Testament scriptures?

Reflect on the words of the Pontifical Biblical Commission on this page.

Jesus came to bring good news to the poor, and release to the captives.

❖ Pray that we may recognise our own poverty before God, and our own need for release from those things which hold us captive.

Jesus is revealed in this story as the prophet for the nations and not simply for God's people Israel.

❖ Pray that we may acknowledge God's grace wherever it may be at work, even beyond the boundaries of the Church.

Jesus' proclamation of the gospel leads to rejection by his own people.

❖ Pray for the strength and courage to proclaim the good news of liberation, even when that might bring rejection, ridicule or hostility.

The Pontifical Biblical Commission writes:

The Gospels and Acts have a basic outlook on Jews that is extremely positive because they recognise that the Jews are a people chosen by God for the fulfilment of his plan of salvation. This divine choice finds its highest confirmation in the person of Jesus, son of a Jewish mother, born to be the Saviour of his people, one who fulfils his mission by announcing the Good News to his people, and by performing works of healing and liberation that culminate in his passion and resurrection. The attachment to Jesus of a great number of Jews, during his public life and after his resurrection, confirms this perspective, as does Jesus' choice of twelve Jews to share in his mission and continue his work.

(The Jewish People and their Sacred Scriptures in the Christian Bible, 70).

Calling his Followers

Hear the Word of God

Read Luke 5:1-16

[1] Once while Jesus was standing beside the lake of Gennesaret, and the crowd was pressing in on him to hear the word of God, [2] he saw two boats there at the shore of the lake; the fishermen had gone out of them and were washing their nets. [3] He got into one of the boats, the one belonging to Simon, and asked him to put out a little way from the shore. Then he sat down and taught the crowds from the boat.

[4] When he had finished speaking, he said to Simon, 'Put out into the deep water and let down your nets for a catch.' 5 Simon answered, 'Master, we have worked all night long but have caught nothing. Yet if you say so, I will let down the nets.' [6] When they had done this, they caught so many fish that their nets were beginning to break. [7] So they signaled their partners in the other boat to come and help them. And they came and filled both boats, so that they began to sink.

[8] But when Simon Peter saw it, he fell down at Jesus' knees, saying, 'Go away from me, Lord, for I am a sinful man!' [9] For he and all who were with him were amazed at the catch of fish that they had taken; [10] and so also were James and John, sons of Zebedee, who were partners with Simon. Then Jesus said to Simon, 'Do not be afraid; from now on you will be catching people.' [11] When they had brought their boats to shore, they left everything and followed him.

[12] Once, when he was in one of the cities, there was a man covered with leprosy. When he saw Jesus, he bowed with his face to the ground and begged him, 'Lord, if you choose, you can make me clean.' [13] Then Jesus stretched out his hand, touched him, and said, 'I do choose. Be made clean.' Immediately the leprosy left him. [14] And he ordered him to tell no one. 'Go,' he said, 'and show yourself to the priest, and, as Moses commanded, make an offering for your cleansing, for a testimony to them.'

[15] But now more than ever the word about Jesus spread abroad; many crowds would gather to hear him and to be cured of their diseases. [16] But he would withdraw to deserted places and pray.

Opposite: Detail from the facade of San Pietro, depicting the calling of Andrew and Simon Peter to become apostles, 12th century.

Understand the Word of God

This session will explore:

- ❖ the call of Simon and its meaning
- ❖ the cleansing of the leper
- ❖ the purpose of miracle stories
- ❖ the message for today

Setting in the Gospel

Luke's focus on the episode in the Nazareth synagogue means that he has delayed until now describing the call of Jesus' first disciples. Matthew and Mark both locate the call of four fishermen at the very beginning of the ministry. We are now ready for the first of Jesus' associates to be identified: Simon Peter.

Up to this point, Luke has described how Jesus left Nazareth behind, and moved to his new base of Capernaum (*Luke* 4:31). There we see him, in the rest of chapter 4, beginning to fulfil the prophecy of Isaiah: setting free a man oppressed by evil powers, healing Simon Peter's mother-in-law, and restoring to wholeness people with a range of diseases.

Christ Calling his Disciples, 1839 by Adam Brenner (1800-91).

This will continue after Simon Peter's call with the cleansing of a leper. The Twelve Jesus begins to gather round him in 6:12-16 will play a special role in continuing this ministry of preaching good news to the poor, and letting the oppressed go free.

What Kind of Text?

This passage contains two very different kinds of story. The first is a call story, describing the dramatic transformation of Simon the fisherman and his associates, James and John, who are mentioned in verse 10. There is a partial parallel in Mark chapter 1 and Matthew chapter 4, both of whom describe in a matter-of-fact way the call of the first four disciples, including Simon Peter's brother Andrew. Jesus passes by and invites them to follow. They leave their fishing business and follow.

Such call stories are probably influenced by Old Testament call narratives such as that of Elisha by Elijah in 1 Kings 19:19-21. But typically, Luke has provided a more detailed and realistic account, bringing out the transforming impact of Jesus on Simon Peter.

Moreover, Luke has interwoven the call story with a 'nature miracle', a miraculous catch of fish. This has striking parallels with the post-resurrection miracle described in John chapter 21. The miracle points to the power of Jesus as Lord, and symbolises the mission of Peter and his associates, whose interest has changed from fish to people.

The second story is a healing story, specifically the cleansing of a leper. Healings were not unique to Jesus in the ancient world. They are attested in both Jewish and non-Jewish sources. But the stories of Jesus' healings and exorcisms focus on his power to act as God's Messiah, bringing in God's kingdom, and overcoming all that stood in the way of that kingdom. They contain similar elements to other ancient stories about healers: a description of the disease or sickness, the action of the healer, and the reaction of the witnesses.

The Plain of Gennesaret spreads out below the Arbel cliffs.

Commentary: verse by verse reading

The Call of Simon Peter

Gennesaret or Ginnosar is the name of a broad plain, and a city overlooking that plain, on the north-western shore of the lake (Matthew 14:34 Mark 6:53). Given Gennesaret's proximity to the water, Lake Galilee was sometimes called the 'lake of Gennesaret', as at Luke 5:1 (and also in 1 Maccabees 11:67).

St Augustine of Hippo comments on this passage:

The nets were cast. They caught so many fish that two boats were filled, and the very nets were torn by that vast quantity of fish. Then he said to them, 'Follow me, and I will make you fishers of men.' They received from him the nets of the Word of God, they cast them into the world as into a deep sea, and they caught the vast multitude of Christians that we can see and marvel at. Those two boats, though, stood for the two peoples, Jews and Gentiles, synagogue and church, those circumcised and those uncircumcised.

(Sermon 248)

v.1 Luke locates the episode by the 'lake of Gennesaret', his title for the inland Sea of Galilee. As a man who has sailed the great Mediterranean, Luke is reluctant to call a freshwater lake a 'sea'. The growing influence of Jesus is denoted by the image of crowds pressing in to hear him teach.

vv.2-3 The reference to the two boats prepares us for the end of the story, when Simon the fisherman will receive a new vocation. There are places around the Sea of Galilee where the curved shore-line forms a natural amphitheatre, enabling someone speaking from a boat a little distance out to be audible. Hence Jesus gets into one of the boats to teach.

vv.4-5 The quality of Simon's faith is revealed in his readiness to put out into the deep and put down the nets again. It is remarkable that this experienced fisherman, who has caught nothing all night, responds positively to this prophet with no apparent knowledge of the fishing industry.

In Luke's sequence of events, the healing of Simon's mother-in-law (4:38-39) has already shown Peter the possibilities that faith in Jesus might bring. Hence he calls Jesus 'Master' (Greek *epistata*, which literally means 'one who stands over'). This title is only found in Luke among the gospels, and always used of Jesus by the disciples who submit to Jesus' authority.

vv.6-7 The miracle performed far outweighs any possible expectations. There are so many fish that the nets are beginning to break. In the parallel account at John 21:11 we are given a number: a hundred and fifty-three. This incredible and unforeseen catch, given the unpromising circumstances, points to the equally remarkable expansion of the church, initially spear-headed by Peter, narrated in the Acts of the Apostles.

v.8 The reaction of Simon is to recognise his own sinfulness and unworthiness to be in Jesus' presence. His address to Jesus is ambiguous: the Greek *Kurie* could simply be a polite form of address, 'Sir'. But it can also mean 'Lord', which Luke probably intends.

For the first time, Luke calls Simon by his double-name Simon Peter, pointing to the transformation which has taken place. Simon (or *Simeon*) is his own name. But the gospels (*Matthew* 16:18 *Mark* 3:16 *Luke* 6:14 *John* 1:42) recount how Jesus gives Simon a new name: *Petros* in Greek or *Kepha* in Aramaic. This name comes from the word for 'rock', perhaps pointing to the new role which the rather weak Peter will play in the post-Easter community.

vv.9-10 As a reminder that this call story is also a miracle story, we learn of the amazement of the onlookers, a typical feature of such texts. James and John are described here as 'partners' (Greek *koinonoi*) with Simon, those who share things in common, in this case, their fishing business. This anticipates the life of the early Jerusalem community in Acts, where the believers had all things in common.

Acts 2:42 and 44 They devoted themselves to the apostles' teaching and fellowship (Greek koinonia), to the breaking of bread and the prayers. All who believed were together and had all things in common. (Greek koina).

Jesus' invitation to Simon is subtly different from that in the other synoptics. There the fishermen are invited to become 'fishers of people' (*Mark* 1:17 and *Matthew* 4:19). But what fishermen do to the fish they catch is hardly salvific! The fish are caught in order to be killed and eaten, not a very appropriate metaphor for the Christian mission. Instead, Luke's Jesus calls the fisherman Peter to 'catch human beings', to take them alive.

v.11 The three fishermen now make that crucial transition from onlooker to disciple. They leave everything and follow him. The urgency of the kingdom is such that some, notably the Twelve, must make this radical step. Yet there are many others in the gospels whom Jesus calls to remain in their own homes, testifying to what the Lord has done (e.g. *Luke* 8:39)

Cleansing a Leper

The term leprosy in the Old Testament and wider ancient world covered a wide range of skin complaints and diseases, including leprosy proper. The background for understanding Jewish regulations about leprosy is Leviticus 13-14. Those Jews with such a condition were pronounced ceremonially unclean by a priest. A priest was also required to pronounce the person clean after the condition had subsided. Leviticus 13:45-46 reads: 'The person who has the leprous disease shall wear torn clothes and let the hair of his head be dishevelled; and he shall cover his upper lip and cry out, 'Unclean, unclean.' He shall remain unclean as long as he has the disease; he is unclean. He shall live alone; his dwelling shall be outside the camp.'

v.12 Luke is fond of rather vague time and place references, as 'when he was in one of the cities'. Nevertheless, the city location is important for this particular story. Lepers were excluded from society, hence Luke's words hint at the separation between this leper and his city. This also explains Jesus' concern in verse 16 to leave the cramped urban environment and escape to a deserted place.

This is one of two stories in Luke which describes the cleansing of lepers. The other, at Luke 17:11-19, concerns ten lepers of whom only one, a Samaritan, returns to give thanks.

The man's reaction to Jesus is one of profound veneration, appropriate to meeting a king or other eminent figure. Again, there is ambiguity in the address *Kurie*: is he addressing Jesus as 'Sir', or acknowledging him as 'Lord'?

v.13 Jesus' total willingness to cleanse the man is striking: 'I do choose. Be made clean.' The language of clean/unclean is cultic rather than ethical. One needs to be ritually clean in order to enter God's temple,

and play a full part in the religious and social life of one's community. We should be careful not to equate being unclean with being a sinner.

Jesus' words are matched by Jesus' actions. It is a matter of debate whether in touching the leprous man, Jesus was risking becoming ritually unclean himself. More important is Jesus' statement: 'Be clean'. According to the Law of Moses, priests had authority to pronounce that someone was clean. Here Jesus is actually rendering the man clean.

v.14 However, Jesus does not disregard the Law, in obedience to which he has been brought up by the law-abiding Mary and Joseph. Rather, he urges the man to go to the priest and offer the prescribed sacrifice, the complicated regulations for which can be found in Leviticus chapter 14.

Mark 1:44 Jesus said: 'See that you say nothing to anyone; but go, show yourself to the priest, and offer for your cleansing what Moses commanded, as a testimony to them.'

One of Mark's characteristic features is to associate Jesus' actions with a note of secrecy, especially commands to silence. Luke has apparently taken this from Mark, by matching the command to offer the sacrifice with an equally stern admonition about telling anyone.

vv.15-16 Unlike Mark, however, Luke makes no suggestion that the leper disobeys this command. Rather, the word is spread around by others, such that Jesus gains a following as a healer. His reaction is to get away from the city, and he withdraws to deserted places. Finally, Luke tells us that Jesus went there to pray. We are given many glimpses of Jesus' intimate moments of prayer in Luke's gospel. He prays at strategic points in his ministry, and this is echoed by the prayer of the Church in Acts.

Luke 6:12 (Jesus prays before calling the apostles) Now during those days he went out to the mountain to pray; and he spent the night in prayer to God.

Luke 9:18 (before the profession of faith by Peter) Once when Jesus was praying alone, with only the disciples near him, he asked them, 'Who do the crowds say that I am?'

Luke 9:29 (at the Transfiguration) And while he was praying, the appearance of his face changed.

Opposite: Christ Heals a Leper, Italian School, (15th century).

The Word Lives on

Luke's version of the call of Peter is unique, but all four gospels recount his call, and his special position within the Twelve.

In John's Gospel, Simon is brought to Jesus directly by his brother Andrew, and given his new name of 'Peter' (*John* 1:42). In Matthew, the naming of Peter takes place at Caesarea Philippi, where Simon acclaims Jesus as 'the Messiah, the Son of the living God' (*Matthew* 16:16).

All three synoptics record the cleansing of the leper, though at different points in the ministry. For Matthew, it is the first thing Jesus does having preached his Sermon on the Mount (*Matthew* 8:1-4).

In the Lectionary

The call of Simon Peter (*Luke* 5:1-11) provides the gospel for the Fifth Sunday in Ordinary Time in Year C. In the Weekday Lectionary, the same passage is read on Thursday of the twenty-second week in Ordinary Time, and the healing of the leper on 11th January.

St. Andrew and St. Peter Responding to the Call of Jesus, from the main nave of Sant'Apollinare Nuovo, Ravenna, Italy. Byzantine School, (6th century).

Live the Word of God

Listen again to the reading: Luke 5:1-16

What do you hear now?

Suggestions for reflection and prayer

What aspects of the story of Simon Peter speak to you in your life of faith?

How do you think we might understand Jesus' words about putting out into deep water?

Reflect on the words of St Augustine, given earlier, on the miraculous catch of fish.

Who are the contemporary lepers in our society? What does Luke's story invite us to do?

Jesus gives Simon a new name.

❖ Pray that we be worthy of the new name we received in baptism.

Simon falls down before Jesus, declaring himself to be a sinner.

❖ Pray that we may recognise our own sinfulness, but also our own worth in Christ's eyes.

Jesus seeks out a deserted place to be by himself and pray.

❖ Pray for a renewed commitment to finding time and space to be with God in prayer.

St Cyprian of Carthage writes:

Not by words alone, but also by deeds has God taught us to pray. He himself prayed frequently and demonstrated what we ought to do by the testimony of his own example. But if he who was without sin prayed, how much more ought sinners to pray, and if he continually prayed, watching through the whole night with uninterrupted petitions, how much more ought we to lie awake at night in continuing prayer!

(The Lord's Prayer 29).

Women Follow Jesus

Hear the Word of God

Read Luke 7:36-8:3

[37] And a woman in the city, who was a sinner, having learned that he was eating in the Pharisee's house, brought an alabaster jar of ointment. [38] She stood behind him at his feet, weeping, and began to bathe his feet with her tears and to dry them with her hair. Then she continued kissing his feet and anointing them with the ointment.

[39] Now when the Pharisee who had invited him saw it, he said to himself, 'If this man were a prophet, he would have known who and what kind of woman this is who is touching him-- that she is a sinner.'

[40] Jesus spoke up and said to him, 'Simon, I have something to say to you.' 'Teacher,' he replied, 'Speak.' [41] 'A certain creditor had two debtors; one owed five hundred denarii, and the other fifty. [42] When they could not pay, he cancelled the debts for both of them. Now which of them will love him more?' [43] Simon answered, 'I suppose the one for whom he cancelled the greater debt.' And Jesus said to him, 'You have judged rightly.'

[44] Then turning toward the woman, he said to Simon, 'Do you see this woman? I entered your house; you gave me no water for my feet, but she has bathed my feet with her tears and dried them with her hair. [45] You gave me no kiss, but from the time I came in she has not stopped kissing my feet. [46] You did not anoint my head with oil, but she has anointed my feet with ointment. [47] Therefore, I tell you, her sins, which were many, have been forgiven; hence she has shown great love. But the one to whom little is forgiven, loves little.'

[48] Then he said to her, 'Your sins are forgiven.' [49] But those who were at the table with him began to say among themselves, 'Who is this who even forgives sins?' [50] And he said to the woman, 'Your faith has saved you; go in peace.'

[8:1] Soon afterwards he went on through cities and villages, proclaiming and bringing the good news of the kingdom of God. The twelve were with him, [2] as well as some women who had been cured of evil spirits and infirmities: Mary, called Magdalene, from whom seven demons had gone out, [3] and Joanna, the wife of Herod's steward Chuza, and Susanna, and many others, who provided for them out of their resources.

Opposite: Christ in the House of Simon the Pharisee, c.1635 by Claude Vignon, (1593-1670

Understand the Word of God

This session will explore:

- ❖ the story of the woman in the Pharisee's house
- ❖ the meaning of hospitality and table-fellowship
- ❖ the place of women followers in Luke's account
- ❖ the message for today

Setting in the Gospel

Since the cleansing of the leper in 5:12-14, Luke's narrative has described increasing opposition to Jesus and his ministry, particularly from religious people such as Pharisees, scribes, and teachers of the law. In contrast, tax-collectors and sinners, a poor widow, even a Gentile centurion, have welcomed the good news.

Things have come to a head immediately before this passage, over the figure of John the Baptist. Luke reminds his readers how the tax-collectors and sinners eagerly welcomed John, and accepted his baptism of repentance. In contrast, the Pharisees and lawyers remained closed to God's offer (7:29-30).

Against this background, a Pharisee called Simon invites Jesus to dine at his house. The story raises this question: will Simon react to Jesus like his fellow Pharisees, or will he respond in a more open way?

Supper in the House of the Pharisee by Peter Rubens (1577-1640).

What Kind of Text?

This passage contains two kinds of texts. The first in Luke 7:36-50 is very similar to the typical Greek *symposium*, where a meal provides the opportunity for discussion and instruction, led by a teacher or philosopher. Hence the story contains an important teaching, the parable of the two debtors in verses 41-43. Meals are significant for Luke as occasions where Jesus breaks down barriers and draws excluded people in, anticipating the great banquet in the kingdom of God. They are also reminders that the Eucharist offers the same opportunity in the life of the Church.

The presence of the woman, and her action of anointing Jesus with ointment, has led many to connect this story with those in the other synoptics, where a woman anoints Jesus' head at Bethany in Matthew 26:6-13 and Mark 14:3-9. In the version in John 12:1-8, Mary of Bethany anoints Jesus' feet and wipes them with her hair, as in Luke. The similarities can be overstressed, however. In the other gospels, the texts come at the beginning of the Passion Narrative and the woman is recognising Jesus as Messiah or 'anointed one', and preparing him for his burial. In Luke the theme is very different: the amazing love and forgiveness of God, and the human response it provokes.

The second passage (8:1-3) is one of Luke's typical summaries of Jesus' ministry. Since the Infancy Narrative, Luke has stressed the role of significant women in the outworking of God's plan. Here we discover that Jesus and the twelve were accompanied on their preaching missions by women of substantial means, who supported them financially. Unlike the woman just mentioned, some of these are mentioned by name: Mary, called Madgalene, Joanna the wife of Chuza, and Susanna.

Despite the juxtaposition of the two stories, there is no suggestion that the woman who anoints Jesus is Mary Magdalene, a connection made in some later traditions.

Commentary: verse by verse reading

The Meal

The Pharisees were one of a number of Jewish groups in first century Palestine, made up of both priests and laymen. The more aristocratic Sadducees are also mentioned in the gospels, unlike the Essenes. 'Pharisee' probably means 'separated', highlighting a concern for ritual purity in everyday life. Although they probably had little political power during Jesus' ministry, by the time Luke writes several decades later the Pharisees have become the dominant leadership of the Jewish community.

v.36 Unlike Matthew, who gives very negative, stereotypical portrayals of characters like the Pharisees, Luke's portrayal is more realistic and three-dimensional. He gives this particular Pharisee an identity and a name, Simon. His description raises the possibility that at least some Pharisees were more favourable towards Jesus than Matthew's depiction suggests. Indeed, Luke depicts Jesus as dining with Pharisees on a regular basis, and in 13:31 tells us of a group of Pharisees going out of their way to warn Jesus that Herod wanted to kill him.

v.37 We only learn that the woman was a sinner. There is no hint as to the nature of her sin, only that it was sufficiently well-known in the city. Given this story's context in Luke's gospel, we should not be surprised to find this sinner responding more favourably to Jesus than his Pharisee host. The depth of her grateful response is hinted at in the perfumed, sweet-smelling ointment.

v.38 Luke envisages that Simon and his guests were reclining on couches in Greek style, with their feet stretched out away from the table. Hence the woman 'stood behind him at his feet'. Ancient readers may well have been shocked by the description of the woman kissing Jesus' feet, in a society where intimate contact between men and women was reserved for married couples and close family relations.

But the thing that David had done displeased the Lord, and the Lord sent Nathan to David. He came to him, and said to him, 'There were two men in a certain city, the one rich and the other poor…'
(2 Samuel 12:1).

vv.39-40 Simon's private thoughts dismiss what the reader knows to be true, that Jesus is a prophet. Ironically, Jesus' prophetic credentials are clear, for he knows both what Simon is thinking and the true depths of the woman's response. Hence, like the prophet Nathan whose parable shocked David into a change of heart (2 *Samuel* 12), Jesus forces a rethink through the parable he tells his host.

vv.41-42 The parable which Jesus tells here, like several of his parables, describes a world in which many were gripped by the burden of debt. Both debtors in the parable owe substantial amounts, given that one denarius represented a day's pay for a labourer. But one of these debtors owed ten times more than the other. This gives Jesus' parable a surprising twist, for few real creditors would write off such large debts as does the one in this story. But God's forgiving love cannot be measured in such human terms.

v.43 Simon's response to Jesus shows that he has understood the general point of the parable: those who have been forgiven more will have greater love. But does he fully understand what that means for him? The fact that there are two debtors in the story suggests that Simon too is a debtor, a sinner in need of forgiveness.

vv.44-46 Ancient Palestinian society took hospitality and its associated rituals very seriously. Jesus' words here reveal that Simon has failed in the basic obligations of hospitality towards his dinner guest, neither providing water for washing his dusty feet on arrival, nor welcoming him with the expected kiss, nor anointing his head with oil. By contrast, in her overwhelming gratefulness for forgiveness received, the woman has performed extravagant acts of hospitality. We are left wondering who is the real host at this party: Simon, or the woman who makes up Simon's lack, or even Jesus.

v.47 This verse gives us the punch-line of the whole story. It both explains the parable and contrasts the extravagance of the woman's response with the half-hearted welcome offered by Jesus' host. The tense of the verb ('her sins, which were many, have been forgiven') tells us that God has already forgiven her, even before Jesus' pronouncement in verse 48. Indeed, her behaviour shows that she has already experienced this forgiveness.

vv.48-50 As in the healing of the paralytic in Luke 5:17-26, Jesus now pronounces the woman's sins forgiven. The Greek verb Luke uses is the same form as in the previous verse, a perfect passive (meaning something like 'have been forgiven and remain so'). However, the reaction of those at table shows that they understand it as Jesus forgiving the woman's sins at that point. Hence the NRSV translation 'Your sins are forgiven'. They are scandalised because Jesus is assuming the role of a priest, who traditionally declared God's forgiveness, or even of God himself. As Jesus has told us in 5:24, he is the Son of Man who has authority on earth to forgive sins.

In Matthew 18:23-35 we read the parable of the Unforgiving Servant, a similar parable about debtors, though focused on human rather than divine forgiveness.

St Ephrem the Syrian writes:

She, through her love, brought into the open the tears that were hidden in the depths of her eyes, and the Lord, because of her courage, brought into the open the thoughts that were hidden in the Pharisee.

(Commentary on Tatian's Diatessaron 7.18).

Jesus' Preaching Tour

v.1 Luke provides one of his typical summaries of Jesus' ministry. Jesus is gathering around him a new or renewed people of God, who are captivated by his message of God's kingdom breaking in. Luke's vision of the kingdom or reign of God has already been glimpsed in Jesus' Nazareth speech: when the oppressed are set free and the poor are raised up. Just as Israel of old had its twelve tribes named after the patriarchs, so too the community around Jesus has a particular group of twelve at its heart.

St Paul writes of his claim to be an apostle:

Am I not free? Am I not an apostle? Have I not seen Jesus our Lord?

(1 Corinthians 9:1)

The gospels all agree that Jesus selected twelve of his followers to perform a special role, even though there is disagreement about the names of some of them. For Luke, the twelve are to be equated with the apostles; for other New Testament writers, especially Paul, the apostles are a wider group than the twelve.

v.2 When Luke describes male characters, he normally balances them with females. Thus he tells us that the group around Jesus consisted not only of the twelve, but also women followers. They have experienced the freedom that the Messiah brings. In the world of Jesus, certain physical and psychological conditions were believed to be due to the activity of evil spirits. Their experience of liberation and wholeness is probably the reason why they now follow Jesus so intensely.

The Magdalen by Perugino, Galleria Palatina, Florence.

Their prominence is shown by the fact that their names have been preserved, unlike several other women in the gospels. The first is Mary Magdalene, from the town of Magdala on the western shore of the Sea of Galilee. Mary is probably the most famous of Jesus' women disciples, who is present in all four gospel accounts of the empty tomb.

v.3 The second woman, Joanna, will accompany Mary Magdalene and some other women to Jesus' tomb, to become among the first witnesses to the resurrection (*Luke* 24:10). Little else is known about her. Her husband Chuza is described as a 'manager' or 'steward' of Herod. This Herod is Herod Antipas, son of Herod the Great, who was tetrarch of Galilee and Perea between 4 BC and 39 AD.

Nothing apart from her name is known about the third woman, Susanna, who is not mentioned again in the New Testament. There are also other unnamed women. These are women of financial means, who minister to Jesus and the male disciples out of their own material resources. The verb translated 'provided for' is the verb from which we get our word 'deacon'.

Mark 16:1 When the Sabbath was over, Mary Magdalene, and Mary the mother of James, and Salome bought spices, so that they might go and anoint him.

Matthew 28:1 After the Sabbath, as the first day of the week was dawning, Mary Magdalene and the other Mary went to see the tomb.

Luke 24:10 Now it was Mary Magdalene, Joanna, Mary the mother of James, and the other women with them who told this to the apostles.

John 20:1 Early on the first day of the week, while it was still dark, Mary Magdalene came to the tomb.

The three women at the tomb, 13th century.

The Word Lives on

As noted, this story of a woman in a Pharisee's house is unique to Luke. The closest parallel is in John 12, where Mary the sister of Martha and Lazarus anointed Jesus' feet and wiped them with her hair. In later Christian tradition, these two stories are often harmonised, along with the quite different story in Matthew and Mark. There is no justification from the text to identify the woman who is a sinner with Mary Magdalene.

More significant is the positive description of Mary Magdalene, Joanna, Susanna and the other women at the end of this passage. This anticipates the role of Mary and the others in the gospel stories of the empty tomb, where they become first witnesses to the resurrection. The Magdalene's role is particularly singled out in the tradition: she becomes the *apostola apostolorum*, the 'apostle to the apostles'.

In the Lectionary

The complete text we have studied provides the gospel for the Eleventh Sunday in Ordinary Time in Year C. In the Weekday Lectionary, it is read on Thursday and Friday of the twenty-fourth week in Ordinary Time.

Alabaster Jar.

Live the Word of God

Listen again to the reading: Luke 7:36-8:3

What do you hear now?

Suggestions for reflection and prayer

How do you react to the actions of the woman? And to the response of Simon the Pharisee?

Reflect upon a situation in which you have experienced forgiveness, or have been asked to show forgiveness to someone who has offended you.

What might this story of the meal in Simon's house teach us about our obligations towards each other at Mass?

What can we learn from the women in this passage about what it means to be a disciple of Christ?

The woman with the jar of ointment showed an embarrassing excess of love towards Jesus.

❖ Pray for the gift of gratitude, to respond to the offer of forgiveness with thankful love.

She caused scandal by kissing Jesus' feet.

❖ Pray for the courage to reach out to others in their need, even at the risk of causing scandal and shock.

Simon failed in his obligation of hospitality towards the Lord.

❖ Pray that we may fulfil our obligations of hospitality, especially towards the stranger, and those unable to repay that hospitality.

From the Catechism of the Catholic Church:

Contemplative prayer is the prayer of the child of God, of the forgiven sinner who agrees to welcome the love by which he is loved and who wants to respond to it by loving even more. (n.2712)

Learning to Pray

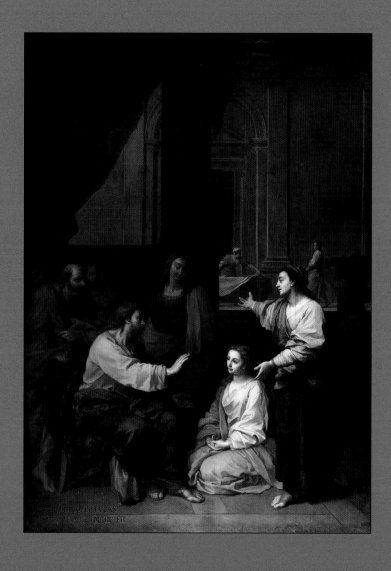

Hear the Word of God

Read Luke 10:38-11:13

[38] Now as they went on their way, he entered a certain village, where a woman named Martha welcomed him into her home. [39] She had a sister named Mary, who sat at the Lord's feet and listened to what he was saying.

[40] But Martha was distracted by her many tasks; so she came to him and asked, 'Lord, do you not care that my sister has left me to do all the work by myself? Tell her then to help me.' [41] But the Lord answered her, 'Martha, Martha, you are worried and distracted by many things; [42] there is need of only one thing. Mary has chosen the better part, which will not be taken away from her.'

[11:1] He was praying in a certain place, and after he had finished, one of his disciples said to him, 'Lord, teach us to pray, as John taught his disciples.' [2] He said to them, 'When you pray, say:

Father, hallowed be your name. Your kingdom come.

[3] Give us each day our daily bread.

[4] And forgive us our sins, for we ourselves forgive everyone indebted to us. And do not bring us to the time of trial.'

[5] And he said to them, 'Suppose one of you has a friend, and you go to him at midnight and say to him, 'Friend, lend me three loaves of bread; [6] for a friend of mine has arrived, and I have nothing to set before him.' [7] And he answers from within, 'Do not bother me; the door has already been locked, and my children are with me in bed; I cannot get up and give you anything.' [8] I tell you, even though he will not get up and give him anything because he is his friend, at least because of his persistence he will get up and give him whatever he needs.

[9] 'So I say to you, Ask, and it will be given you; search, and you will find; knock, and the door will be opened for you. [10] For everyone who asks receives, and everyone who searches finds, and for everyone who knocks, the door will be opened.

[11] Is there anyone among you who, if your child asks for a fish, will give a snake instead of a fish? [12] Or if the child asks for an egg, will give a scorpion? [13] If you then, who are evil, know how to give good gifts to your children, how much more will the heavenly Father give the Holy Spirit to those who ask him!'

Opposite: Christ with Martha and Mary by Claude Saint-Paul, (1666-1716)

Understand the Word of God

This session will explore:

- ❖ the story of Mary and Martha
- ❖ Luke's teaching about prayer
- ❖ the petitions of the Lord's Prayer
- ❖ the message for today

Setting in the Gospel

Examples of the prayer of the disciples in Luke and Acts:

Luke 24:52-53 They worshipped him, and returned to Jerusalem with great joy; and they were continually in the temple blessing God.

Acts 1:14 All these were constantly devoting themselves to prayer, together with certain women, including Mary the mother of Jesus, as well as his brothers.

Acts 2:42 They devoted themselves to the apostles' teaching and fellowship, to the breaking of bread and the prayers.

Acts 3:1 Peter and John were going up to the temple at the hour of prayer.

At this point in Luke, Jesus is on his long final journey to Jerusalem, which dominates the central section of this gospel (9:51-19:28). Jerusalem plays a crucial role for Luke, and his opening and closing scenes both occur there. Jerusalem is the holy city where the Christ must suffer. Jerusalem is the place from where Christ is to ascend to glory. Meanwhile, the journey to Jerusalem provides Jesus with the opportunity for a wide range of teaching, sayings and encounters. It is along the journey of faith, 'day by day' and little by little along the way, that Jesus' disciples learn what it means to follow him.

These two episodes, one an encounter with Mary and Martha and the other a dialogue between Jesus and his disciples, are set early on the journey. Their common theme is that of attentiveness to God, whether through listening to God's word or learning how to pray effectively. The prayer of Jesus and his followers is an important theme running throughout Luke and Acts.

What Kind of Text?

The first story in 10:38-42 describes an episode at the house of Mary and Martha which is unique to Luke. It is what New Testament scholars call a pronouncement story, a narrative which climaxes in an important statement or pronouncement from Jesus, found in verse 42 in this story. The details of the story are less important than the pronouncement itself.

The second episode provides a good example of Jesus' teaching about prayer. It combines a fragment of liturgy, the Lord's Prayer, with a parable about a night-time visitor, and additional teaching about petitionary prayer.

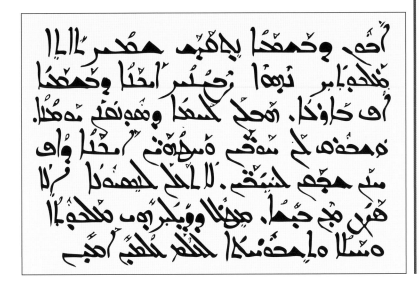

The Lord's Prayer in Aramaic.

Commentary: verse by verse reading

Mary and Martha

v.38 In this whole section of the journey to Jerusalem, Luke is often imprecise about time and place: 'Now as they went on their way'. The village is unnamed, and the fact that Luke locates this event early in the journey would suggest a village in Galilee or Samaria, or perhaps the Jordan valley.

In John's Gospel, however, the sisters Mary and Martha, together with their brother Lazarus, live in Bethany, a village near Jerusalem (*John* 11:1). Bethany is too close to Jerusalem for Luke's purposes. Jesus does not arrive in that area until Luke chapter 19. However, both Luke and John suggest a close, almost familial relationship between Jesus and the two sisters.

What is perhaps most surprising about Luke's account is that the women dominate. There is no mention of Lazarus. Instead, Martha plays the role of the host in welcoming Jesus. Some ancient manuscripts of the gospel emphasise her hospitality by adding the words 'into her home'.

Christ in Martha's House by Giovanni da Milano (14th cent.)

v.39 Mary is mentioned second. The name Mary was a common one for Jewish women, a form of Miriam, the name of Moses' sister. Luke stresses Mary's posture, sitting at the Lord's feet. This is a position of a disciple, who recognises a teacher's authority and sits to learn from him. She is literally listening to 'his word', which is what Christ asks of all his disciples.

v.40 By contrast, Martha is distracted. She has turned a good thing, her service (Greek *diakonia*), into something which gets in the way of hearing Christ's word. Indeed, her hyperactivity leads her to criticise her sister.

vv.41-42 Here we come to the pronouncement, where Jesus reveals the real problem. He is the guest and Martha the host. But in her business in the kitchen, perhaps to lay on a good spread, she is neglecting the more basic rules of hospitality. She should be devoting her attention to him and his word. That is 'the one thing necessary', which Mary has recognised.

Luke 8:21

But he said to them: 'My mother and my brothers are those who hear the word of God and do it.'

St Augustine of Hippo writes:

At present alleluia is for us a traveller's song, but this tiresome journey brings us closer to home and rest where, all our busy activities over and done with, the only thing that will remain will be alleluia. That is the delightful part that Mary chose for herself, as she sat doing nothing but learning and praising, while her sister, Martha, was busy with all sorts of things. Indeed, what she was doing was necessary, but it was not going to last.

(Sermon 255)

Kitchen Scene with Christ in the House of Martha and Mary, by Diego Rodriguez de Silva y Velazquez c.1618.

The Lord's Prayer

v.1 The next scene gives us one of Luke's glimpses of Jesus at prayer. In Matthew chapter 6, the Lord's Prayer is taught as part of the Sermon on the Mount, and in a longer form. Luke has Jesus teach the prayer on the journey to Jerusalem, and at the request of one of his disciples. Set forms of prayer (e.g. the Eighteen Benedictions) had already begun to develop in the synagogue. In addition, specific Jewish groups had their own forms or patterns of prayer. The disciples of John the Baptist do so. Jesus' followers want their own.

In the Bible, the name expresses the character of a person, their true self. God is holy, and to sanctify his name is also to accept his invitation to become holy, as he is holy. See Leviticus 11:45.

v.2 The prayer is addressed to God as 'Father'. While praying to God as Father is known within Jewish prayer, this prayer reflects Jesus' practice of addressing God by the intimate Aramaic 'Abba'. In Christian prayer, we dare to call God 'Father' as Jesus does. Like our Jewish brothers and sisters, we also pray for the hallowing of God's name.

Some manuscripts expand verse 2 to make it agree with Matthew. Still others add 'May your Holy Spirit come upon us and cleanse us.' While this is certainly an addition by a later scribe, it is in keeping with Luke's overall vision: just as Jesus fulfils his ministry in the power of the Holy Spirit, so we need to be transformed by the Spirit in order to share his healing work.

The second petition is a prayer that God's kingdom may break into human lives. Since Jesus' Nazareth sermon, we have seen plenty of examples of this in his ministry. Jesus' followers must pray that they may cooperate with that kingdom, rather than obstructing its progress.

But how often should we pray for this bread? Matthew's version emphasises what we need now: 'Give us today'. Luke's wording recognises that we need this sustenance at every stage of our Christian journey: 'keep on giving us, day by day'.

v.3 The first two petitions were directed towards God. The final three focus on human beings. The first is a request for bread, the staple diet of most people in the ancient world, and therefore a powerful symbol of basic human need. The precise meaning of the word translated 'daily' (Greek *epiousios*) is unclear. It could mean 'the bread we need to exist', acknowledging our utter dependence on God for our physical needs. Other possibilities include 'our bread for today' (like the manna in the wilderness, *Exodus* 16), and 'our bread for the future' (the bread of the Messiah's banquet). The Fathers sometimes understood it as a reference to the Eucharist.

John Cassian (c. 360-435) writes:

With 'daily' the Evangelist shows that without this bread we cannot live a spiritual life for even a day. When he says 'this day', he shows that the bread must be eaten each day. It will not be enough to have eaten yesterday unless we eat similarly today. May our daily poverty encourage us to pour out this prayer at all times, for there is no day on which it is unnecessary for us to eat this bread to strengthen the heart of the person within us.

(Conference 9.21)

v.4 Throughout Luke, God is presented as compassionate and forgiving. Thus Jesus teaches his disciples to pray for forgiveness for their own sins. But his followers are also to be marked by the same spirit of forgiveness.

The final petition may echo Old Testament memories of God bringing his people to the point of testing or trial, particularly the temptation to apostasy (as in the wilderness after the Exodus). This language is intelligible within an ancient worldview in which God is in total control, and which does not distinguish as we do between God causing certain things and God permitting them to happen. Some think that Jesus is referring to the final trial that was expected to precede the messianic age.

Further Teaching about Prayer

vv.5-6 The Lord's Prayer contains both praise and petition. The remainder of this passage offers teaching specifically on petitionary prayer. It begins with a parable, drawn from everyday life, in which a man wakes up his friend in the middle of the night in order to borrow bread to feed an unexpected visitor. Luke's readers would hear echoes of the Lord's Prayer with its petition for daily bread. In this story, however, the request is not made for the man's own needs, but for the sake of another.

v.7 On one level, the reaction of the friend woken in the middle of the night is understandable. He is concerned about the rest of the family being disturbed, in a smallish house with a communal sleeping area. But the obligations of hospitality and the rules of friendship override such considerations: he owes it to his friend to plunder the larder and provide the bread.

v.8 Here we come to the punch-line. What persuades the reluctant householder to act is his friend's stubborn persistence or 'shamelessness'. Jesus will similarly commend the widow's persistence at Luke 18:1-8. There is both a similarity and a contrast drawn between this householder and God. God is utterly committed to us as is a man to his friend. Yet God never refuses to act on that commitment.

vv.9-10 From our side, the parable emboldens us to pray with confidence, even with persistence. This is reiterated in the next few verses. The sequence of passive verbs ('it will be given you', 'the door will be opened for you') is a biblical way of saying that God does the giving and the opening. They express the conviction that, despite appearances to the contrary, all true prayer is heard and answered.

vv.11-13 Another contrast is now set up between human fathers and the God whom Jesus has taught us to call Father. If even a human father would not dream of giving his son a snake instead of a fish, or a scorpion instead of an egg (*Matthew* 7:9 has a stone instead of bread), our heavenly Father is even more generous. Our Father loves us far more than any human parent, showering us with the greatest gift possible: the Holy Spirit (*Matthew* 7:11 has 'good things').

In the Sermon on the Mount in Matthew's gospel Jesus says:

'Is there anyone among you who, if your child asks for bread, will give a stone? Or if the child asks for a fish, will give a snake? If you, then, who are evil, know how to give good gifts to your children, how much more will your Father in heaven give good things to those who ask him!'

(Matthew 7:9-11)

The Word Lives on

The story of Mary and Martha is unique to Luke, although details of their lives have been filled out by appeal to John's Gospel, where they appear alongside their brother Lazarus. The episode Luke describes has continued to inform later Christian theology and spirituality. In particular, it has often been used to explore the differences between the contemplative and active forms of the religious life. The scene has often been painted by artists (e.g. Diego Velázquez's Christ in the House of Martha and Mary).

Matthew's parallel account of the Lord's Prayer has focused on its immediate, End-time character: we are bidden to pray for God's kingdom to come urgently. It also has a strong liturgical ring: we pray this prayer as a community at worship: Our Father.

Luke's probably later version might be prayed by an individual ('Father'), and acknowledges that we need to pray and seek the kingdom 'day by day' throughout the journey of our lives. Of course, the Lord's Prayer has continued to play a central role in Christian prayer and liturgy, both at Mass and at Morning and Evening Prayer, although Matthew's version rather than Luke's has been the favourite.

Saints of different centuries, such as Cyprian and Teresa of Avila, have left us writings which invite us to meditate on the prayer, one petition at a time.

In the Lectionary

In the Sunday Lectionary, the story of Martha and Mary (Luke 10:38-42) provides the gospel for the Sixteenth Sunday in Ordinary Time in Year C, with Luke 11:1-13 being set for the following Sunday. The complete text we have studied is read on Tuesday, Wednesday and Thursday of the twenty-seventh week in Ordinary Time.

Live the Word of God

Listen again to the reading: Luke 10:38-11:13

What do you hear now?

Suggestions for reflection and prayer

What do you see as the difference between Martha's and Mary's responses to Jesus?

Meditate on the two versions of the Lord's Prayer in Matthew chapter 6 and Luke chapter 11. How does each one speak to you?

Reflect on the words about the Lord's Prayer from the Catechism of the Catholic Church given below.

Mary learned to sit and listen at the feet of Jesus.

❖ Pray for the wisdom to recognise the one thing necessary, and not be overwhelmed by the distractions of daily life.

Jesus taught us to pray for the coming of God's kingdom.

❖ Pray that we may be instruments of God's liberating rule, and never obstruct its progress.

The man in the parable sought his friend in the middle of the night.

❖ Pray for the gift of perseverance in prayer, particularly when it feels difficult or seems ineffective.

Finally, if we pray Our Father sincerely, we leave individualism behind, because the love that we receive frees us from it. The 'our' at the beginning of the Lord's Prayer, like 'us' of the last four petitions, excludes no one. If we are to say it truthfully, our divisions and oppositions have to be overcome.

(Catechism of the Catholic Church n.2792)

The Prodigal Son

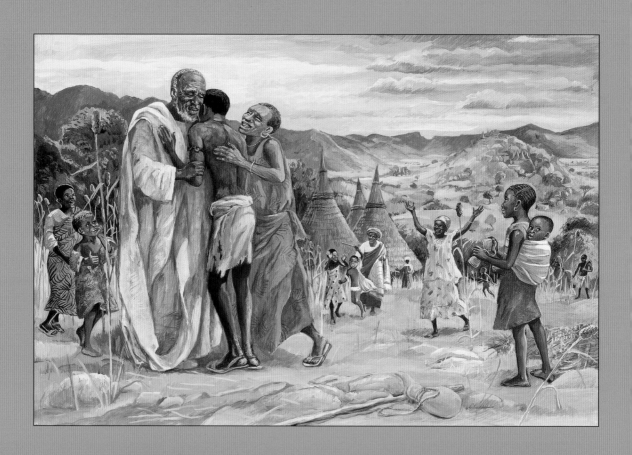

Hear the Word of God

Read Luke 15:11-32

[11] Then Jesus said, 'There was a man who had two sons. [12] The younger of them said to his father, 'Father, give me the share of the property that will belong to me.' So he divided his property between them.

[13] A few days later the younger son gathered all he had and travelled to a distant country, and there he squandered his property in dissolute living. [14] When he had spent everything, a severe famine took place throughout that country, and he began to be in need. [15] So he went and hired himself out to one of the citizens of that country, who sent him to his fields to feed the pigs. [16] He would gladly have filled himself with the pods that the pigs were eating; and no one gave him anything.

[17] But when he came to himself he said, 'How many of my father's hired hands have bread enough and to spare, but here I am dying of hunger! [18] I will get up and go to my father, and I will say to him, 'Father, I have sinned against heaven and before you; [19] I am no longer worthy to be called your son; treat me like one of your hired hands.' '

[20] So he set off and went to his father. But while he was still far off, his father saw him and was filled with compassion; he ran and put his arms around him and kissed him. [21] Then the son said to him, 'Father, I have sinned against heaven and before you; I am no longer worthy to be called your son.' [22] But the father said to his slaves, 'Quickly, bring out a robe-- the best one-- and put it on him; put a ring on his finger and sandals on his feet. [23] And get the fatted calf and kill it, and let us eat and celebrate; [24] for this son of mine was dead and is alive again; he was lost and is found!' And they began to celebrate.

[25] 'Now his elder son was in the field; and when he came and approached the house, he heard music and dancing. [26] He called one of the slaves and asked what was going on. [27] He replied, 'Your brother has come, and your father has killed the fatted calf, because he has got him back safe and sound.' [28] Then he became angry and refused to go in. His father came out and began to plead with him.

[29] But he answered his father, 'Listen! For all these years I have been working like a slave for you, and I have never disobeyed your command; yet you have never given me even a young goat so that I might celebrate with my friends. [30] But when this son of yours came back, who has devoured your property with prostitutes, you killed the fatted calf for him!'

[31] Then the father said to him, 'Son, you are always with me, and all that is mine is yours. [32] But we had to celebrate and rejoice, because this brother of yours was dead and has come to life; he was lost and has been found."

Opposite: The Prodigal Son by Jesus Mafa

Understand the Word of God

This session will explore:

- ❖ Luke's use of parables
- ❖ the setting of this parable in Luke's story
- ❖ the characters of the two sons, and their father
- ❖ the message for today

Setting in the Gospel

Jesus' journey to Jerusalem continues, with a succession of teachings, debates and healings. In 12:1 Luke numbers the pilgrim crowds around him in the thousands.

At this point, Jesus is confronted with the grumblings of the Pharisees and scribes, objecting to his association with tax collectors and sinners (15:1-2). In response to these murmurings, Jesus tells three parables, all describing the search for something lost: the lost sheep (15:4-7), the lost coin (15:8-10), and this lengthy parable of the lost son (15:11-32).

We normally call this story the 'prodigal son' (a title found in English Bibles since the sixteenth century), referring to the son's squandering of his share of the inheritance. Others suggest 'the parable of the two sons', or 'the parable of the forgiving father', for it is he who stands at the centre of the story.

What Kind of Text?

This is one of the longest and most famous of Luke's parables, which has inspired artists and preachers as well as biblical commentators. Parables are a familiar feature of Jesus' teaching as recorded in the synoptic gospels, stories which often surprise and force us to see the world differently. Luke's parables are particularly memorable for their literary skill, dramatic twists and psychological insight into the complexity of human lives. In this parable, Luke offers a lengthy narrative which is both memorable and challenging to the reader. It gives us keen insight into Luke the storyteller, and through him, into Jesus, the master storyteller.

Matthew's parable of the two sons has some similarities:

'What do you think? A man had two sons; he went to the first and said, 'Son, go and work in the vineyard today.' He answered, 'I will not'; but later he changed his mind and went. The father went to the second and said the same; and he answered, 'I go, sir'; but he did not go. Which of the two did the will of his father?'

(Matthew 21:28-31)

The Return of the Prodigal Son by Rembrandt, (1606-1669).

Commentary: verse by verse reading

The Younger Son's Journey

v.11 The story seems to presuppose a wealthy Jewish landowner with two sons. Neither his daughters nor, more surprisingly given the ensuing story, his wife are mentioned. The concentration on the two sons echoes Israel's history, which contains several stories exploring the relationship between male siblings, such as Isaac and Ishmael, Jacob and Esau, and Joseph and his brothers.

But the present context in Luke, as seen earlier in verses 1-2, suggests that the younger son represents the tax collectors and sinners, and the elder son the grumbling Pharisees and scribes. There is an irony here, in that sons ought to recognise one another as brothers and equals. As the parable progresses, however, we detect a touch of sibling rivalry. In particular, the elder son resents the unconditional love and compassion poured out on his undeserving younger brother.

v.12 The father does not simply divide his possessions between the sons. He divides his very life (Greek *bios*), all he had to live on. In Luke 21:4 the word *bios* is used in a similar way of the poor widow, who 'put in all she had to live on'. Jewish inheritance laws allowed a father to dispose his property either after his death or during his life-time, as he does in the parable. Since the firstborn inherited a double share (*Deuteronomy* 21:17), the younger son would have received a third of the inheritance.

v.13 We are not told where the far country to which the prodigal son journeyed was, although journeying to distant and exotic places is a regular feature of stories of discovery.

Jews in the first century lived in a number of distant lands, the result of emigration and exile. But we are not told whether the young man in the story went to some far-flung part of the Jewish diaspora. What we do know is that he ends up far from his family home, and from the holy land. There he squanders his inheritance, though Luke is silent about the nature of his dissolute living.

Deuteronomy 21:17

He must.............give the firstborn a double portion of all that he has; since he is the first issue of his virility, the right of the firstborn is his.

v.14 Famine is a common feature of the biblical world, reflecting the harsh conditions under which Middle Eastern agricultural societies operate.

v.15 Hiring himself out to one of the citizens expresses the depths into which the younger son has descended. Sons are essentially free. As long as he remained in his father's house, the prodigal son would have retained his freedom. Now, however, he has become a hired servant, and hired to a foreigner at that. Losing his filial relationship with his father has lost him his own identity.

v.16 Jesus' Jewish audience would have been particularly horrified to learn that he was reduced to working with pigs, and even willing to eat the carob pods on which they were fed. Pigs were considered unclean, and avoidance of pork was a clear stipulation of the Law of Moses. Not only has he ceased to be a son of his father, but he has also ceased to be a son of Israel.

v.17 At the lowest point in the story, transformation begins to take place. Having travelled to a far country, and been stripped of everything in which he invested worth, the younger son 'came to himself'.

Jesus, himself on a journey to Jerusalem as he tells this parable, teaches us that the journey is often the means to self-discovery, of bringing us back to where we began with new insight. Even here, however, there is a hint of jealousy as well as regret, as the son remembers how even hired hands are treated in his father's house. He still has some way to go on his journey.

vv.18-19 As he embarks on his interior journey back to being a son, the young man rehearses a speech which has strong echoes of the Lord's Prayer. It is addressed to his 'Father', and contains an admission of sin which calls for forgiveness. He has come to see the truth with clarity: 'I am no longer worthy to be called your son.' His prayer also acknowledges how our relationship with God is intimately bound up with our relationship with other human beings: 'I have sinned against heaven (against God) and before you.'

In Genesis 12:10 we read: 'Now there was a famine in the land. So Abram went down to Egypt to reside there as an alien, for the famine was severe in the land.' In Genesis chapter 42 it is because of famine that Jacob sends his sons into Egypt, where they encounter their brother Joseph. The book of Ruth begins: 'In the days when the judges ruled, there was famine in the land, and a certain man of Bethlehem in Judah went to live in the country of Moab, he and his wife and two sons.' (Ruth 1:1)

Leviticus 11:7 explains why pigs are considered unclean:

The pig, for even though it has divided hoofs and is cleft-footed, it does not chew the cud; it is unclean for you.

The Return

Genesis 33:4 But Esau ran to meet him, and embraced him, and fell on his neck and kissed him, and they wept.

Genesis 45:14-15 Then he fell upon his brother Benjamin's neck and wept, while Benjamin wept upon his neck. And he kissed all his brothers and wept upon them; and after that his brothers talked with him.

v.20 The extravagant action of the father, quite shocking to those who first heard this parable, is to run ahead and meet his son while still far off, rather than waiting with the expected dignity for him to approach. He is 'filled with compassion', a Greek term which expresses emotion at the very depths of one's being.

When we are told that he 'put his arms around him' (literally 'fell upon his neck'), we might be reminded of Esau's embrace of his brother Jacob (*Genesis* 33:4), or Joseph's reconciliation with Benjamin and his other brothers (*Genesis* 45:14-15).

vv.21-22 The son begins his well-rehearsed speech. Yet it is as though the father has not heard it, and he does not allow him to finish the words he had rehearsed ('treat me like one of your hired hands').

Instead, the father requests several gifts normally given to an honoured guest or prominent member of the household. The best robe suggests a festal garment. A ring was not just an item of jewellery but a sign of authority. Sandals would be worn by sons and guests of honour, but never by slaves.

v.23 The greatest sign of honour is the calf 'fattened up with grain', which is what Luke's Greek implies, rather than grazed on grass. This would have been very expensive, and therefore kept in reserve for a very special occasion. In 1 Samuel 28:24 we read how the witch of Endor prepares the fatted calf for king Saul.

In Luke 22:28 Jesus says to the disciples:

'You are those who have stood by me in my trials; and I confer on you, just as my Father has conferred on me, a kingdom, so that you may eat and drink at my table in my kingdom.'

v.24 The response of the father picks up, like a refrain, the reaction of the shepherd to finding the lost sheep ('I have found my sheep that was lost' verse 6) and the woman to locating her lost coin ('I have found the coin that I had lost' verse 9). In both cases, the reaction reflected heaven's (that is, God's) joy at the repentance of a sinner. The emphasis upon eating and celebrating echoes the promised banquet of the Kingdom of God.

The Story of the Elder Son

v.25 The previous verse might have been a good place to end the parable. But for Luke the character of the elder son is equally crucial, particularly in the context of Jesus' debate with the Pharisees and scribes (verses 1-2). He too has a place in his father's heart. So the final part of this dramatic parable focuses on him and his response.

vv.26-27 The elder son relies upon a second hand report, that of a slave, rather than entering his own house to discover for himself the reason for the music and dancing. This offers a hint that it is not only the younger son who has become estranged from his father.

The Prodigal Son, 1975-76 by Marc Chagall, (1887-1985).

v.28 Whereas the younger son experienced sorrow, the elder experiences anger, which prevents him from making the much shorter journey home. The context of the parable should remind us of the resentment of the Pharisees and scribes towards Jesus' scandalously lax attitude towards the tax collectors and sinners (verses 1-2). But the father's role remains consistent: he now comes out to meet his elder son also. If the father's compassion enabled the return of the younger son, it is equally at work in the rehabilitation of the older son who remained.

v.29 Luke provides great insight into motivations behind duty, and even religious practice. The elder brother views himself more as a slave of his father than a son. He does not even see his relationship as equal to the hired hands who worked for his father (verse 17).

The son's resentment is expressed in his reproach that his father has never even given him a goat to share with his friends. A goat (or in some manuscripts a 'kid') would have been considerably cheaper than a fatted calf.

v.30 In his resentment, the elder son is only too ready to specify the sins of his younger brother: 'This son of yours has devoured your property with prostitutes.' That this is his speculation seems confirmed by Luke's reluctance to specify in verse 13.

v.31 In the words of the father the laws of inheritance are again invoked: 'All that is mine is yours.' Now that the younger has squandered his share, all that the father has belongs to his elder son.

v.32 What the father wishes his elder son to see is that the return of the prodigal is like a return from the dead, which restores the family so that the estranged younger son is once again 'this brother of yours'. Christian hearers of this parable could not fail to hear resonances of Jesus' resurrection: 'he was dead and has come to life'.

Unlike the previous parables of the lost sheep and lost coin, this parable does not end with an explicit interpretation. But that is because the interpretation has been breaking in throughout. Though the father of the two sons is not God (the younger son has sinned both against God and his own father), he provides a powerful vision of what our Father is like.

The real question posed by the parable is: how will the story end? We do not learn how the elder son responded to his father's words, nor indeed the ultimate fate of the younger son.

Just as this parable ends with unresolved tension, so does the parable of the fig tree which Luke narrates in 13:6-9. At the end of the parable we do not know whether the owner of the vineyard will allow the fig tree one more year.

The Word Lives on

This parable is unique to Luke's gospel, and is rich in themes popular with Luke, such as mercy, forgiveness and the reversal of roles. There may be some overlap with Matthew's parable of the two sons (*Matthew* 21:28-32), but if so Luke has reshaped it into something quite distinctive. It has been immensely influential in the history of the Church.

Early commentators, understanding Luke to be the gospel for the Gentiles, interpreted the elder son as Israel and the younger as the Gentiles, or as the Church. The dramatic journey of the prodigal, and the compassionate welcome of the father, have inspired countless artists. Rembrandt's Return of the Prodigal Son is perhaps the most famous, but Albrecht Dürer, Hans Sebald Beham, Francesco Bassano and Giovanni Francesco Barbieri have also depicted the parable.

Peter Chrysologus writes:

'He had two sons,' that is, two peoples, the Jews and the Gentiles. Prudent knowledge of the law made the Jewish people his older son, and the folly of paganism made the Gentile world his younger son.

(Sermon 5).

In the Lectionary

The Prodigal Son, together with Luke's introduction to chapter 15 (*Luke* 15:1-3, 11-32), is read on the Fourth Sunday of Lent in Year C. The whole of Luke 15, including the parables of the Lost Sheep and Lost Coin, is read on the Twenty-Fourth Sunday in Ordinary Time in Year C. In the Weekday Lectionary, this passage is set for Saturday in the Second Week in Lent.

Live the Word of God

Listen again to the reading: Luke 15:11-32

What do you hear now?

Suggestions for reflection and prayer

Reflect on the words of Pope John Paul II given below.

Which of the characters do you most readily identify with? The younger son? The elder son? The father? Does your answer change as the story progresses?

The younger son went on a journey to a far country.

❖ Pray that we may discover ourselves more deeply in our journey of faith.

The father ran out to meet his son with compassion.

❖ Pray that we may receive God's offer of forgiveness, which affirms our dignity as children of God.

The elder son refused to welcome his brother.

❖ Pray that our treatment of our brothers and sisters may not be obscured by resentment, jealousy or anger.

Pope John Paul II writes:

We read, in fact, that when the father saw the prodigal son returning home 'he had compassion, ran to meet him, threw his arms around his neck and kissed him'. He certainly does this under the influence of a deep affection, and this also explains his generosity towards his son, that generosity which so angers the elder son. Nevertheless, the causes of this emotion are to be sought at a deeper level. Notice, the father is aware that a fundamental good has been saved: the good of his son's humanity. Although the son has squandered the inheritance, nevertheless his humanity is saved. Indeed, it has been, in a way, found again.

(Dives in Misericordia IV.6)

The Rich Man and Lazarus

Hear the Word of God

Read Luke 16:19-31

[19] 'There was a rich man who was dressed in purple and fine linen and who feasted sumptuously every day.

[20] And at his gate lay a poor man named Lazarus, covered with sores, [21] who longed to satisfy his hunger with what fell from the rich man's table; even the dogs would come and lick his sores.

[22] The poor man died and was carried away by the angels to be with Abraham. The rich man also died and was buried. [23] In Hades, where he was being tormented, he looked up and saw Abraham far away with Lazarus by his side. [24] He called out, 'Father Abraham, have mercy on me, and send Lazarus to dip the tip of his finger in water and cool my tongue; for I am in agony in these flames.'

[25] But Abraham said, 'Child, remember that during your lifetime you received your good things, and Lazarus in like manner evil things; but now he is comforted here, and you are in agony. [26] Besides all this, between you and us a great chasm has been fixed, so that those who might want to pass from here to you cannot do so, and no one can cross from there to us.'

[27] He said, 'Then, father, I beg you to send him to my father's house-- [28] for I have five brothers-- that he may warn them, so that they will not also come into this place of torment.'

[29] Abraham replied, 'They have Moses and the prophets; they should listen to them.' [30] He said, 'No, father Abraham; but if someone goes to them from the dead, they will repent.' [31] He said to him, 'If they do not listen to Moses and the prophets, neither will they be convinced even if someone rises from the dead.'

Opposite: The Rich Man in Hell, illustration for 'The Life of Christ', c.1886-94, by James Tissot, (1836-1902).

Understand the Word of God

This session will explore:

❖ the context of this parable in Luke's story

❖ the characters of the rich man and Lazarus

❖ ancient beliefs about life after death

❖ the message for today

Setting in the Gospel

We are now a little further along the journey towards Jerusalem and the cross. Jesus has just told a parable about a dishonest steward (*Luke* 16:1-9), and a series of sayings about wealth have been addressed to the Pharisees who are described as being 'lovers of money' (16:14). This is an unflattering stereotype, for elsewhere Luke tells us of individual Pharisees who are positive towards Jesus, as in Luke 13:31 when some Pharisees warn Jesus of threats against him.

The focus here seems to be on those who use religious piety as a cover for self-gain. The Pharisees are rigorous interpreters of the Law of Moses. Yet how does their practice match up to the 'law and the prophets' (16:16)? Having raised this question, Luke's Jesus now tells the parable of the rich man and Lazarus.

What Kind of Text?

The story of the rich man and Lazarus is another of Luke's vivid narrative parables. Similar tales of reversal of fortunes after death can be found in Egyptian and Jewish sources. Luke's version falls into two parts.

The first part (verses 19-26) explores the gospel theme of reversal, already described in the Magnificat and the Beatitudes. As the latter put it, the poor and hungry are blessed, because their dire situation will be reversed in the kingdom of God; the rich, however, have had their consolation now (*Luke* 6:20-26).

In the second part (verses 27-31), attention is focused on the rich man's brothers, and whether they will repent even if someone should rise from the dead.

Lancet Window depicting the Parable of Lazarus and the Rich Man. French School, (13th century) / Saint-Etienne Cathedral, Bourges, France.

Commentary: verse by verse reading

The Rich Man and Lazarus

v.19 The story begins without an introduction, and Jesus continues to teach. First the rich man is introduced in vivid terms. Purple was the colour of royalty, made from the expensive dye of the murex shellfish. Fine linen undergarments complete his costly clothing. He also 'feasted sumptuously', not just on special occasions, but every day!

v.20 The contrast between the rich man and his poor counterpart could not be starker. But Luke's story has an interesting twist. In conventional stories, the rich and influential take centre stage, while the poor and powerless stand on the margins and remain unnamed. In this parable, however, we are told the name of the poor figure by the gate, while the rich man remains anonymous.

Lazarus is the Greek form of the Hebrew Eleazar, which appropriately enough means 'God has helped'. Even if no human being comes to his assistance, God will act on his behalf. The traditional name of his wealthy opposite, Dives, is simply the Latin for 'rich man'.

St Augustine wrote:

Jesus kept quiet about the rich man's name and mentioned the name of the poor man. The rich man's name was thrown around, but God kept quiet about it. The other's name was lost in silence, and God spoke it. Please do not be surprised. God just read out what was written in his book … You see, God who lives in heaven kept quiet about the rich man's name, because he did not find it written in heaven. He spoke the poor man's name, because he found it written there, indeed he gave instructions for it to be written there.

(Sermon 33A.4)

The Rich Man and Lazarus by Jesus Mafa.

A number of features accentuate Lazarus' pitiful state. He is probably a cripple, as he has literally been 'thrown' beside the rich man's gate. He receives nothing from the extravagant waste of the rich man's sumptuous banquets. For Jews, dogs were unclean animals (*Exodus* 22:31), so his being licked by them adds insult to injury. He is an utter outcast. Shocking though this story may be, it reflects the social and economic inequality of ancient society, and indeed of many modern societies, where the gulf between the richest and the poorest is vast.

Exodus 22:31 'You shall be people consecrated to me; therefore you shall not eat any meat that is mangled by beasts in the field; you shall throw it to the dogs.'

v.22 That Lazarus is carried away by the angels suggests that no human bothered to bury his body. This is a shameful fate for a Jew, as Tobit 1:17 testifies. This parable gives us one of those rare glimpses of Jewish beliefs about life beyond death. It envisages two places or states for the dead, a place of rest and a place of torment, perhaps in that in-between period prior to the resurrection of the dead.

In Tobit 1:17 the exiled Tobit says:
'If I saw the dead body of any of my people thrown out behind the wall of Nineveh, I would bury it.'

Lazarus is safe 'in Abraham's bosom' (translated in the NRSV as 'with Abraham'). Abraham is the primary ancestor for Jews. The phrase the 'bosom' or 'lap' of Abraham is not found in the Bible outside Luke. It is probably linked to the Old Testament expression 'being gathered to one's people', found, for example, in Genesis 49:33 and Deuteronomy 32:50. Reclining on his bosom, or sitting on his lap, suggests not only closeness to the patriarch but having an honoured place with him at table. In John's gospel, the beloved disciple has a similar place of honour close to Jesus at the last supper (*John* 13:23). Lazarus now shares what was refused him during his lifetime, a place at table in a banquet with the patriarchs.

Genesis 49:33 When Jacob ended his charge to his sons, he drew up his feet into the bed, breathed his last, and was gathered to his people.
Deuteronomy 32:50 (The Lord said to Moses) You shall die there on the mountain that you ascend and shall be gathered to your kin.
John 13:23 One of his disciples – the one Jesus loved – was reclining next to him.

v.23 The rich man, meanwhile, is in torment, separated from those things in which he invested so much during his life. Though on an initial reading Hades might appear to be a separate realm from the 'bosom of Abraham', it is more likely that Hades is understood as containing both the blessed and the wicked in different areas, separated by a great chasm.

This fits the Hades of classical mythology, the Greek place of the dead. In the Greek Old Testament, however, 'Hades' is sometimes used for the Old Testament Sheol, a rather shadowy half-life for the departed.

Genesis 37:35 (Jacob said) No, I shall go down to Sheol to my son, mourning.
Psalm 6:5 For in death there is no remembrance of you; in Sheol who can give you praise?

The revelation to the rich man, perhaps a member of the aristocratic Sadducee party, is that Sheol is not quite so shadowy. He finds his Sadducee beliefs challenged. There is judgement after death. There are rewards after death. There is more than a nebulous half-life after death.

v.24 The rich man and Lazarus have one thing in common: they can call upon father Abraham. But the rich man's prayer betrays the selfishness and arrogance which led him to overlook the poor man while alive. Although he knows Lazarus' name, an indication that he was aware of this poor man at his gate during his lifetime, he still thinks of him as his servant who might cool his tongue with a drop of water. Indifferent to Lazarus in life, he remains self-absorbed in death.

v.25 Abraham's reply is a statement of gospel reversal which runs throughout Luke's gospel. The rich man now experiences the woes of the Beatitudes (*Luke* 6:24-26). However, it is not merely that he was rich, but that his riches fostered indifference towards Lazarus, which seems to lie at the heart of this reversal.

v.26 The great chasm between the comforted and agonising dead reflects the chasm that the rich man set up between himself and Lazarus during his lifetime. Our choices in this world affect our position in the next. The rich man's torment is not what God has inflicted on him so much as what he has inflicted on himself.

The Fate of the Rich Man's Brothers

v.27-28 Still thinking of Lazarus as his servant, the rich man now casts him in the role of messenger who should go and warn his brothers. Perhaps they too share the Sadducee view of Sheol as a shadowy state which fails to differentiate between the blessed and the unrighteous. At least they can be allowed to put things right before their own deaths.

v.29 Abraham's response is that they have all they need in 'Moses and the prophets'. 'Moses' refers to the five books traditionally attributed to him, the Pentateuch or Torah. The 'prophets' include both what we call the historical books (*Joshua-2 Kings*, known by Jews as the 'Former Prophets') as well as the main prophetic writings (the 'Latter Prophets').

The main point seems to be this: both the Pentateuch and the prophets proclaim the necessity of social justice, of caring for the weak and vulnerable among God's people. Were the brothers to heed this call, they would not be in danger of the fate of the rich man.

vv.30-31 The rich man's response, and especially Moses' final words, contain unmistakable allusions to the resurrection of Christ from the dead. Readers of Luke would probably detect a criticism here of contemporary Jews, for their failure to accept Christian claims for the resurrection of Jesus.

St Jerome wrote:

Do you now see what Abraham means? You do well to wait for him who will rise from the dead, but Moses and the prophets proclaim that he is the One who is going to rise from the dead. Christ, in fact, speaks in them. If you hear them, you will also hear him.

(On Lazarus and Dives 86)

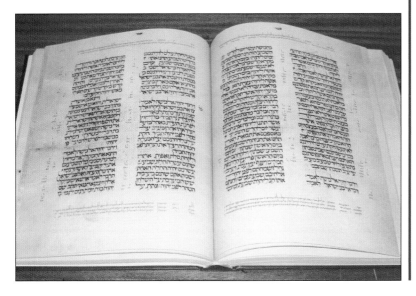

Hebrew Bible.

The Word Lives on

This is another parable which is only found in Luke's gospel. There are, however, some interesting overlaps with John. Luke's parable ends with a conversation between the rich man and Abraham, over whether Lazarus should come back from the dead to warn his brothers. In John 11, we hear the story of a Lazarus who does indeed come back from the dead.

Luke's parable has had a strong influence in art (e.g. Veronese), music (e.g. Vaughan Williams, and his work of 1939 'Dives and Lazarus' for harp and string orchestra) and poetry (e.g. Richard Crashaw).

Rich Lazarus! richer in those gems, thy tears,
Than Dives in the robes he wears:
He scorns them now, but oh they'll suit full well
With the purple he must wear in hell.

(Richard Crashaw, Steps to the Temple 1646).

The Death of Lazarus and the Rich Man, from a capital in the nave, c.1150, French School, (12th century) / La Madeleine, Vezelay, France.

In the Lectionary

The Sunday Lectionary provides this parable as the gospel for the Twenty-Sixth Sunday in Ordinary Time in Year C. It is also set in the Weekday Lectionary for Thursday of the Second Week in Lent.

Live the Word of God

Listen again to the reading: Luke 16:19-31

What do you hear now?

Suggestions for reflection and prayer

Where do you locate yourself in the story of the rich man and Lazarus?

Reflect on the words of St Augustine about the name of Lazarus and the rich man earlier in the commentary.

The rich man left Lazarus at the gate of his house.

❖ Pray that we may have eyes to see the needs of those near to us, and the grace to respond generously.

Lazarus rested in the bosom of Abraham.

❖ Pray for a greater understanding between all those who call upon Abraham, our father in faith.

The rich man's brothers possessed Moses and the prophets.

❖ Pray for a deeper love of the scriptures, and an attentiveness to God's word revealed in them.

We read in Gaudium et Spes, the Pastoral Constitution on the Church in the Modern World of the Second Vatican Council:

Everybody should look upon his or her neighbour (without any exception) as another self, bearing in mind especially their neighbour's life and the means needed for a dignified way of life, lest they follow the example of the rich man who ignored Lazarus, who was poor. (n.27)

The King Enters his City

Hear the Word of God

Read Luke 19:28-44

28 After he had said this, he went on ahead, going up to Jerusalem.

29 When he had come near Bethphage and Bethany, at the place called the Mount of Olives, he sent two of the disciples, 30 saying, 'Go into the village ahead of you, and as you enter it you will find tied there a colt that has never been ridden. Untie it and bring it here. 31 If anyone asks you, 'Why are you untying it?' just say this, 'The Lord needs it."

32 So those who were sent departed and found it as he had told them. 33 As they were untying the colt, its owners asked them, 'Why are you untying the colt?' 34 They said, 'The Lord needs it.' 35 Then they brought it to Jesus; and after throwing their cloaks on the colt, they set Jesus on it. 36 As he rode along, people kept spreading their cloaks on the road.

37 As he was now approaching the path down from the Mount of Olives, the whole multitude of the disciples began to praise God joyfully with a loud voice for all the deeds of power that they had seen, 38 saying, 'Blessed is the king who comes in the name of the Lord! Peace in heaven, and glory in the highest heaven!'

39 Some of the Pharisees in the crowd said to him, 'Teacher, order your disciples to stop.' 40 He answered, 'I tell you, if these were silent, the stones would shout out.'

41 As he came near and saw the city, he wept over it, 42 saying, 'If you, even you, had only recognised on this day the things that make for peace! But now they are hidden from your eyes. 43 Indeed, the days will come upon you, when your enemies will set up ramparts around you and surround you, and hem you in on every side. 44 They will crush you to the ground, you and your children within you, and they will not leave within you one stone upon another; because you did not recognise the time of your visitation from God.'

Opposite: Jesus Christ entering Jerusalem. From 'The Benedictional of St Aethelwold', c. 971-c. 984 by Godeman (d. 984).

Understand the Word of God

This session will explore:

- ❖ the context of this story
- ❖ the meaning of the entry into Jerusalem
- ❖ Jesus' weeping over the city
- ❖ the message for today

Setting in the Gospel

After Luke's lengthy travel narrative, Jesus finally arrives on the outskirts of Jerusalem, and enters the holy city. In the previous chapter (*Luke* 18:31-34) he has told his disciples of his impending passion, death and resurrection, and how that would fulfil the prophets. He has also underscored the disciples' inability to understand his words.

Luke has traced the last steps of Jesus' journey, from the Jordan valley into Jericho, where he healed a blind man (18:35-42) and transformed the life of the rich tax collector Zacchaeus (19:1-10). Immediately before our passage, Jesus told the parable of the pounds, which warns of the rejection of a new king by his servants. Now we see the king entering his capital, to begin the events through which the Son of Man is to suffer, and so enter his glory.

What Kind of Text?

The first section of the passage (verses 28-40) describes Jesus' triumphal entry into Jerusalem, an event described by all four evangelists. It is perhaps best understood as an acted prophecy, with a pronouncement story (verse 39-40) attached.

The Old Testament prophets sometimes acted out prophecies dramatically, to make a greater impact and challenge people to explore their meaning. When Jesus rides down the Mount of Olives on a colt, therefore, his disciples and the crowds are invited to ask what this action means.

This event is followed by Jesus' weeping over Jerusalem, the holy city (*verses* 41-44), a passage only found in Luke's gospel. Again, Israel's prophets provide Jesus with his model. The prophet Jeremiah wept over Judah and Jerusalem (*Jeremiah* 13:17), a reflection of God's own tears for his chosen people (*Jeremiah* 9:1).

Jeremiah 13:17
But if you will not listen,
my soul will weep in secret for your pride;
my eyes will weep bitterly and run down with tears,
because the Lord's flock has been taken captive.

Jeremiah 9:1
'O that my head were a spring of water,
and my eyes a fountain of tears,
so that I might weep day and night for the slain of my poor people!'

Christ Enters Jerusalem,
Ethiopian School, (18th century).

Commentary: verse by verse reading

The Triumphal Entry

v.28 Jesus' purposeful movement towards Jerusalem, which has been a major theme of Luke's narrative since Jesus 'set his face' towards the city at 9:51, is reiterated for the last time.

Jerusalem – built as a city that is bound firmly together.
To it the tribes go up,
the tribes of the Lord,
as was decreed for Israel,
to give thanks to the name of the Lord. (Psalm 122:3-4)

It is crucial for Luke that the Saviour suffers and dies in the holy city, the city of so much sorrow, but also of so many divine promises. The phrase 'going up' reflects the physical ascent to the city, particularly from Jericho far below in the Judean desert. It is also the traditional language of the psalms, sung by pilgrims 'going up' to the house of the Lord, the temple. Indeed, in Luke, this is the first place that Jesus will visit on entering the city (*Luke* 19:45-48).

v.29 The two villages of Bethphage and Bethany are located on the Mount of Olives, across the Kidron valley to the east of Jerusalem and the temple.

Bethphage (probably meaning 'house of unripe figs') is not referred to elsewhere in the Bible outside this story.

Luke 24:50-51:

Then he led them out as far as Bethany, and, lifting up his hands, he blessed them. While he was blessing them, he withdrew from them and was carried up into heaven.

Bethany ('house of Ananiah') is mentioned more frequently, as a village where Jesus lodged (*Matthew* 21:17 and *Mark* 11:11), and where his anointing took place in the house of Simon the leper (*Matthew* 26:6 and *Mark* 14:3). According to John 11:1, Bethany was the village of Lazarus, Mary and Martha. For Luke, it will also be the place from where Jesus ascends into heaven (*Luke* 24:50).

On that day his feet shall stand on the Mount of Olives, which lies before Jerusalem on the east; and the Mount of Olives shall be split in two from east to west by a very wide valley; so that one half of the Mount shall withdraw northward, and the other half southward. … Then the Lord my God will come, and all the holy ones with him.

(Zechariah 14:4, 5b)

The Mount of Olives was believed to play a crucial role in the events of the end, on the basis of a prophecy in Zechariah 14. That is why many pious Jews wish to be buried there, to await the resurrection.

v.30 Jesus' command to his two disciples to bring the colt from the village opposite reveals his prophetic foreknowledge. Since the episode at Nazareth in Luke chapter 4, Luke has portrayed the Messiah as also the great prophet. Now we see the prophet at work once again. Jesus specifies that this is a colt which 'has never been ridden'. It is fit for a king to ride.

v.31 The response the disciples are to give to anyone who asks is nicely ambiguous: 'The *Kurios* needs it'. This Greek word could mean simply master, which is how it is translated in verse 33. But Luke surely wants us to recognise that Jesus is 'the Lord', a second meaning of *Kurios*. This is one of his favourite titles for Jesus, even during his earthly ministry.

vv.32-34 It is important for Luke that the disciples find everything as Jesus told them. This is the pattern of prophecy and fulfilment. Jesus' words are being put on a par with Old Testament prophecy, and so their accurate fulfilment is important. This explains the repetition here of the details in verses 30-31.

Luke 7:13 When the Lord saw her (the widow of Nain), he had compassion for her.

Luke 10:1 After this the Lord appointed seventy others and sent them on ahead of him in pairs.

Luke 10:41 But the Lord answered her: 'Martha, Martha, you are worried and distracted by many things.'

Luke 22:61 The Lord turned and looked at Peter.

The Triumphant Entry into Jerusalem by Jesus Mafa.

v.35 Unlike Matthew and Mark (where Jesus sits himself on the colt), Luke tells us that the disciples sat Jesus on it, having covered it with their cloaks. They have recognised that this is the entry of the king into his city, so they 'enthrone' him. They put the king on his colt, a rather humble substitute for a royal charger.

v.36 Yet Luke also seems to be anxious that we do not misunderstand the nature of Jesus' kingship. He tells us nothing about the people waving branches, a feature found in Matthew, Mark and John. They simply follow the disciples' example by spreading their cloaks on the road, echoing what was done to the new king Jehu at 2 Kings 9:13.

Some scholars explain this omission on the grounds that the waving of branches was associated with Judean nationalistic hopes. Luke then is keen to warn against viewing Jesus as a military Messiah, a king who would drive out the Roman occupiers by force.

v.37 The path down from the Mount of Olives would lead into the Kidron valley, from where Jesus would ascend into the city and the temple from the east. Note that it is the 'whole multitude of the disciples' rather than the crowds as a whole which sings God's praises.

This suggests, on the one hand, that Jesus has been successful in persuading people to become his disciples (a word meaning 'those who learn'). We are then to understand 'the disciples' to be a much larger group than 'the twelve', Jesus' inner core of disciples.

The reason for their singing is 'all the deeds of power that they had seen'. This is a reference to Jesus' miracles, which have been performed throughout his ministry. A number of them have been witnessed on his journey to Jerusalem, the last one in Jericho where Jesus healed the blind man (Luke 18:35-42). In the synoptic gospels, the miracle stories often result in the people praising God.

v.38 The first part of the disciples' words are a phrase from Psalm 118:26, one of the Hallel psalms used to greet pilgrims to Jerusalem at the feasts of Passover and Tabernacles. In Luke's version 'the one who comes' has become explicitly identified as 'the king'.

Praise of God for the miracles of Jesus:

Mark 2:12 They were all amazed and glorified God, saying, 'We have never seen anything like this!'

Matthew 15:31 The crowd was amazed when they saw the mute speaking, the maimed whole, the lame walking, and the blind seeing. And they praised the God of Israel.

Luke 18:43 All the people, when they saw it, praised God.

The second part of their chant is unique to Luke. It is closely modelled on the song of the angels at the annunciation to the shepherds (*Luke* 2:14). The child born to bring peace 'on earth' now at the end of his earthly life brings peace 'in heaven', peace with God from his people.

vv.39-40 This is the last time that the Pharisees are mentioned in Luke's gospel. Despite their antagonism towards Jesus during his ministry, they play no role in the story of his passion and death. Here they attempt to have Jesus' disciples silenced. Jesus' reply about stones crying out is ambiguous.

It might mean that, should the disciples be silenced, the very fabric of the city walls would continue their song. But there is another possibility, suggested by an Old Testament prophecy, Habakkuk 2:11. In Habakkuk, the stones are not crying out for joy, but in protest at corruption and violence. Jesus might be saying: either the king is to be acclaimed by his people, or judgement will inevitably fall on the city which rejects him.

Habakkuk 2:11:

The very stones will cry out from the wall,

and the plaster will respond from the woodwork.

Jesus weeps over Jerusalem

vv.41-42 Although the disciples have just praised God for the gift of 'peace in heaven', Jerusalem is not ready to receive it. In one of the most beautiful but tragic passages in Luke, Jesus weeps over the city. His tears seem to be tears of sorrow and grief for the city he loves, tinged with regret at Jerusalem's inability to see her Lord coming to her.

Lamentations 1:2

She weeps bitterly in the night, with tears on her cheeks.

Lamentations 2:18

Cry aloud to the Lord! O wall of daughter Zion!

Let tears stream down like a torrent day and night!

Give yourself no rest, your eyes no respite!

In weeping over Jerusalem, Jesus stands in an ancient tradition. As seen earlier, Jeremiah imitated God himself in his tears for the city (*Jeremiah* 9:1; 13:17). Nehemiah wept over the ruined state of Jerusalem (*Nehemiah* 1:4). In the Book of Lamentations, Jerusalem weeps for herself and for her exiled children (*Lamentations* 1:2 and 2:18).

We are reminded here that, although Jesus is born as the prince of peace, he is also 'a sign that will be opposed' *(Luke* 2:34). The world finds it hard to accept this gift of peace. As we shall see in the story of his passion, even his own people will be divided over him. Jesus himself has already alluded to this along the road to Jerusalem: 'Do you think that I have come to bring peace to the earth? No, I tell you, but rather division!' *(Luke* 12:51).

vv.43-44 The precise military vocabulary in these verses has suggested to many that Luke recounts Jesus' words in the knowledge of what happened to Jerusalem in 70 AD, with a Roman siege of Jerusalem, culminating in the destruction of the city and the temple. If so, he is keen to show that the words of the prophet Messiah have been fulfilled in history.

Wisdom 3:7 uses the same two Greek words to speak of the 'time' when God 'visits' the righteous to reward them:

In the time of their visitation they will shine forth,

And will run like sparks through the stubble.

Tragically, Jerusalem did not recognise the time (Greek *kairos*) of her 'visitation' (Greek *episcope*). Although the words 'from God' are not found in the original Greek, 'visitation' is a biblical word for God's coming to his people, which can be experienced as either judgement or salvation.

The Word Lives on

Luke's version of the triumphal entry is drawn from Mark 11:1-10. Luke follows Mark closely, except for his occasional changes already noted in the commentary. The scene is of course dramatically re-enacted during the liturgy of Palm Sunday, as well as being a favourite of artists.

Hymns based on the entry into Jerusalem include 'All glory, laud and honour' and 'Ride on, ride on in majesty'. Jesus' weeping over Jerusalem is only found in Luke, but remains a poignant scene. On the Mount of Olives today stands the beautiful little church of Dominus Flevit ('The Lord wept'), commemorating this event. Above the altar is a window, with a host and chalice at its centre, which looks out onto the old city of Jerusalem.

'Wide view of old city', modern day Jerusalem.

In the Lectionary

The first section of this passage (*Luke* 19:28-40) is read at the Blessing of the Palms before the Palm Sunday procession in Year C. Luke 19:41-44 is read on Thursday of the thirty-third week in Ordinary Time.

Palm Sunday celebrations in Israel.

Live the Word of God

Listen again to the reading: Luke 19:28-44

What do you hear now?

Suggestions for reflection and prayer

What images do you have of power and royalty? How does this story challenge those images?

Meditate on the words below from the poet and preacher John Donne (1572-1631).

The two disciples were sent to the village ahead of them to do the Lord's will.

❖ Pray for the courage to follow the Lord, especially in the events of his suffering and death.

Jesus wept over the holy city of Jerusalem.

❖ Pray for the peace of Jerusalem, and for its divided religious communities.

The holy city did not recognise the time of its visitation.

❖ Pray for greater openness to God's coming to us, and forgiveness for those times when we impede God's offer of salvation.

John Donne wrote this about the phrase 'Jesus wept', found here as well as in the story of the raising of Lazarus in John 11:35:

The tears of the text are as a spring, a well, belonging to one household, the sisters of Lazarus;

the tears over Jerusalem are as a river, belonging to a whole country;

the tears upon the cross are as the sea, belonging to all the world;

and though literally there fall no more into our text than the spring, yet because the spring flows into the river, and the river into the sea, and that wheresoever we find that Jesus wept, we find our text, (for our text is but that, Jesus wept) therefore by the leave and light of his blessed Spirit, we shall look upon those lovely, those heavenly eyes, through this glass of his own tears, in all these three lines, as he wept here over Lazarus, as he wept there over Jerusalem, as he wept upon the cross over all of us. For so often Jesus wept. (Sermon XIII).

The Trial before
Pilate and Herod

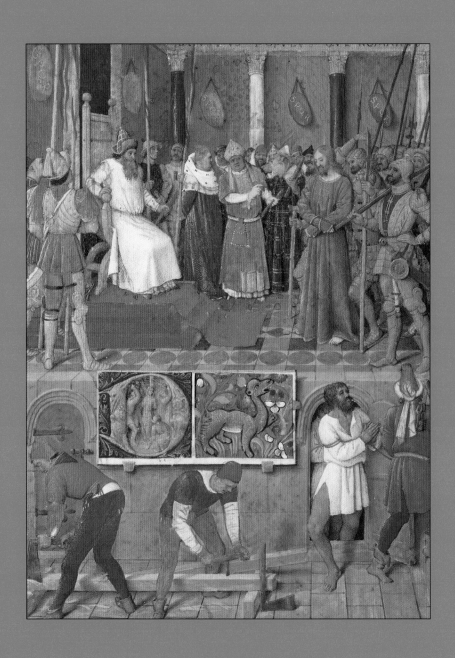

Hear the Word of God

Read Luke 23:1-25

[1] Then the assembly rose as a body and brought Jesus before Pilate. [2] They began to accuse him, saying, 'We found this man perverting our nation, forbidding us to pay taxes to the emperor, and saying that he himself is the Messiah, a king.'

[3] Then Pilate asked him, 'Are you the king of the Jews?' He answered, 'You say so.' [4] Then Pilate said to the chief priests and the crowds, 'I find no basis for an accusation against this man.' [5] But they were insistent and said, 'He stirs up the people by teaching throughout all Judea, from Galilee where he began even to this place.'

[6] When Pilate heard this, he asked whether the man was a Galilean. [7] And when he learned that he was under Herod's jurisdiction, he sent him off to Herod, who was himself in Jerusalem at that time. [8] When Herod saw Jesus, he was very glad, for he had been wanting to see him for a long time, because he had heard about him and was hoping to see him perform some sign. [9] He questioned him at some length, but Jesus gave him no answer. [10] The chief priests and the scribes stood by, vehemently accusing him. [11] Even Herod with his soldiers treated him with contempt and mocked him; then he put an elegant robe on him, and sent him back to Pilate. [12] That same day Herod and Pilate became friends with each other; before this they had been enemies.

[13] Pilate then called together the chief priests, the leaders, and the people, [14] and said to them, 'You brought me this man as one who was perverting the people; and here I have examined him in your presence and have not found this man guilty of any of your charges against him. [15] Neither has Herod, for he sent him back to us. Indeed, he has done nothing to deserve death. [16] I will therefore have him flogged and release him.'

[18] Then they all shouted out together, 'Away with this fellow! Release Barabbas for us!' 19 (This was a man who had been put in prison for an insurrection that had taken place in the city, and for murder.) [20] Pilate, wanting to release Jesus, addressed them again; [21] but they kept shouting, 'Crucify, crucify him!'

[22] A third time he said to them, 'Why, what evil has he done? I have found in him no ground for the sentence of death; I will therefore have him flogged and then release him.' [23] But they kept urgently demanding with loud shouts that he should be crucified; and their voices prevailed.

[24] So Pilate gave his verdict that their demand should be granted. [25] He released the man they asked for, the one who had been put in prison for insurrection and murder, and he handed Jesus over as they wished.

Opposite: Jesus before Pilate, from The Hours of the Cross and the Holy Spirit, from the 'Heures d'Etienne Chevalier', c.1445, by Jean Fouquet (c.1420-80).

Understand the Word of God

This session will explore:

- ❖ the origins of the passion narrative
- ❖ Luke's portrayal of the Roman and Jewish authorities
- ❖ the story of Herod's involvement
- ❖ the message for today

Setting in the Gospel

Since his arrival in Jerusalem and entry into the temple, Jesus has been teaching there, echoing his visit there many years before as a twelve year old (*Luke* 2:41-51). He has been tested by the religious authorities (*Luke* 20:1—47), and has taught again about the destruction of the temple and the holy city (21:5-36).

At the beginning of Luke 22, the story of the passion has begun, with a succession of connected stories moving us towards the cross, resurrection and ascension, the goal of Jesus' journey to Jerusalem. So far, Luke has told us the story of Judas' betrayal, the last supper, Jesus' arrest in Gethsemane and his appearance before the Sanhedrin. In this passage, we join the story as Jesus is taken from the high priest's palace to the Roman governor, Pontius Pilate.

What Kind of Text?

The passion narrative, of which this section is part, has a very different feel from the rest of the gospel. It is made up of a series of connected events, and locates them in a very precise chronological framework. It also draws heavily on allusions to the Old Testament, particularly the prophets and psalms, to make sense of the events of the Passion. For these reasons many scholars think that the passion narrative was the earliest part of the gospel tradition to be written down. Some suggest that its origins lie in retelling the story of Jesus' passion, death and resurrection during the liturgy.

Luke's version overlaps with that in Matthew and Mark, though it also goes its own way at specific points, and there are some striking similarities with John's passion narrative.

This particular section raises important historical questions about responsibility for Jesus' crucifixion. As Luke tells the story, perhaps to reassure the authorities that Christianity was not a politically dangerous movement, Pilate appears more positive than the Jewish authorities. Yet historically it was the Romans, not the local Jewish aristocracy, who had authority to impose the death penalty.

Jesus before Pilate, a mosaic at the Church of Sant' Apollinare Nuovo, Ravenna, Italy.

Commentary: verse by verse reading

The Accusations before Pilate

v.1 'The whole assembly' or 'all the multitude' seems to be the Sanhedrin (22:66), made up of members of the leading priestly families ('the chief priests') and scribes. These Jewish aristocrats would have had particular responsibility for the temple and other internal Jewish matters. But ultimate political authority in Judea and Samaria, including the city of Jerusalem, lay with the Roman governor or prefect. This had been the case since Rome deposed Herod the Great's son, Archelaus, in 6 AD. Pontius Pilate held the office of prefect between 26 and 36 AD.

v.2 The accusations against Jesus in Luke are quite distinctive, and focus on the political dimension of his messiahship. Leading Israel astray, the sign of a false prophet, is a charge made against Jesus in later rabbinic literature. Earlier in Luke (20:20-26), Jesus had been questioned over paying tribute to the emperor, but his ambiguous answer there does not warrant the charge that he forbade paying such taxes.

Luke 19:37-38 The whole multitude of the disciples began to praise God joyfully with a loud voice for all the deeds of power that they had seen, saying, 'Blessed is the king who comes in the name of the Lord!'

The identification of Jesus as Israel's royal Messiah, the Son of David, is presented in terms intended to worry Rome. Jesus is accused of claiming to be a king, that is, a rival to Caesar. In fact, it was Jesus' disciples who acclaimed Jesus as king, at 19:37-38.

v.3 Historians are fairly confident that Pilate's question here describes the charge on which Jesus was executed: that he was a rival king. The Romans reserved crucifixion to a small number of groups: common criminals, slaves, and rebels against the Roman state. Jesus as king clearly falls into the latter category. Yet Luke is keen to underscore Jesus' ambivalence about this title. Hence his reply to Pilate: 'You say so'.

vv.4-5 The dialogue contrasts Pilate's reluctance to convict Jesus with the insistence of Jesus' own people that he is a trouble-maker. Notice how the chief priests have now been joined by 'the crowds', extending the Jewish opposition to Jesus beyond the rulers. Luke's more positive portrait of Roman authority needs to be treated with care when reconstructing the historical events.

Pilate finds Jesus innocent three times:

Luke 23:4 I find no basis for an accusation against this man.

Luke 23:14 I have not found this man guilty of any of your charges against him.

Luke 23:22 I have found in him no ground for the sentence of death.

Christ Before Pilate, c.1530 by Lodovico Mazzolino, (c.1479-c.1528).

Jesus and Herod

vv.6-7 This episode of Jesus' appearance before Herod is only found in Luke's gospel. Herod is Herod Antipas, son of Herod the Great, who ruled Galilee and the territory of Perea east of the Jordan from 4 BC to 39 AD. He is the Herod responsible for the beheading of John the Baptist (*Luke* 3:18-19; 9:9). Herod has presumably come south to Jerusalem for the pilgrimage festival of Passover. Because Jesus is a Galilean, from Nazareth, Pilate sends him to Herod.

Isaiah 53:7 has this to say of the Servant of the Lord: He was oppressed, and he was afflicted, yet he did not open his mouth; like a lamb that is led to the slaughter, and like a sheep that before its shearers is silent, so he did not open his mouth.

vv.8-9 The portrait of Herod here is not particularly flattering. We have already heard that he wanted to see Jesus (*Luke* 9:9). Yet he is one of those who seek signs for their own sake (*Luke* 11:30), viewing Jesus as little more than a magician to perform for their entertainment. Jesus' refusal to give Herod a sign is matched by his refusal to answer his questions. Luke portrays Jesus as the Servant of the Lord, who suffers on behalf of the people (*Isaiah* 53:7).

v.10 Luke links this event with the main trial by the presence of the chief priests and scribes, accusing Jesus.

v.11 Despite recognising Jesus' innocence, Herod is no better than them in his contemptuous mocking of Jesus. Luke lacks the story of Jesus being mocked by the Roman soldiers, found in the other three gospels. Instead it is a Jewish ruler and his troops who mock the Jewish Messiah. The 'elegant robe' (Greek *lampros* meaning 'white' or 'radiant') is probably a mock royal robe.

St Ambrose of Milan writes:

Herod and Pilate, who became friends instead of enemies through Jesus Christ, symbolise the peoples of Israel and the Gentiles, since the future harmony of both follows from the Lord's passion.

(Exposition of the Gospel of Luke 10.103)

v.12 The result of this encounter is that the rivals Herod Antipas and Pilate make peace with each other. We have an ironic hint of the gospel message: repentance, forgiveness and reconciliation of enemies.

Jesus is handed over to Crucifixion

vv.13-15 Luke again presents Pilate in a more favourable light than the religious authorities. He refuses to accept that Jesus is guilty. In Matthew's gospel, this is accompanied by Herod washing his hands in Matthew 27:24. Further, Pilate interprets Herod's return of Jesus as evidence that Herod also found him innocent of the charges against him. The innocence of Jesus is a major theme of Luke's passion story.

Precise reactions and motives of the parties involved in Jesus' last hours on earth are difficult to untangle from these later accounts. They are interwoven with reflection on the Old Testament and influenced by later tensions between Jews and Christians. Christians therefore need to act with the utmost care in drawing historical conclusions from a passage such as this.

v.16 Pilate's proposal is to have Jesus flogged and then released. Roman flogging was a brutal enough punishment, inflicting a great deal of pain and ripping the flesh.

v.17 This verse is left out of the NRSV translation given above because it is missing from several important manuscripts of Luke, and may well have been added by a scribe to explain verse 18, under the influence of Matthew 27:15 and Mark 15:6. It describes the tradition of the Romans releasing a prisoner at the Passover. Such a tradition is not attested outside the gospels. However, it would not be an inappropriate gesture for Passover, which is a feast celebrating Israel's release from captivity in Egypt.

Verse 17 reads: Now he was obliged to release someone for them at the festival.

vv.18-21 The culpability of the leaders is accentuated in the gospels by their choice of Barabbas over Jesus. Nothing is known of Barabbas apart from the gospels. His name in Aramaic means 'son of the father', an irony which would not have been lost on early Christians. Luke tells us that he had committed 'murder', linked to an insurrection in the city. In contrast to the Messiah who offers peace, Barabbas is associated with violence and death.

vv.22-23 Three-fold repetition is common in ancient literature, and effectively reinforces a point. In the gospels, examples include Jesus' three-fold prayer in Gethsemane, and the three times that Peter denies Jesus. Here Pilate's verdict of Jesus' innocence is mentioned for a third time, as is the people's reaction.

vv.24-25 Luke stresses how Pilate gives in to the request of the Jewish leadership for Jesus to be crucified, and reiterates the crimes of Barabbas. The reaction of the religious authorities will immediately be contrasted with that of other Jews, who respond to Jesus with compassion: Simon, a North African from Cyrene in Libya (verse 26), and the weeping women of Jerusalem (verses 27-28).

John 18:31 Pilate said to them, 'Take him yourselves and judge him according to your law.' The Jews replied, 'We are not permitted to put anyone to death.'

The phrase 'he handed Jesus over as they wished' is difficult historically, for it implies that the Jewish authorities carried out Jesus' crucifixion. As John tells us (*John* 18:31), only the Romans had the power to carry out such a death penalty in Judea at this time. Luke is again accentuating the role of the Jewish leadership.

Isaiah 53:6 All we like sheep have gone astray; we have all turned to our own way, and the Lord has laid on him the iniquity of us all.

But 'hand over' has a deeper theological sense. In Isaiah 53:6, the Lord is said to have handed over the suffering Servant for our sins. Throughout the passion story, although humans play their part, the evangelists stress that ultimately God's will is done.

Opposite: Christ before Pilate by Pietro Lorenzetti, (1280-c. 1348).

The Word Lives on

The scene involving Herod is, as has already been noted, unique to Luke. But much of this section, including the dramatic encounter between Jesus and Pontius Pilate, is described – albeit with differences – in all four gospels. Particular interest has been paid to Pilate's motives in allowing Jesus to be crucified. The encounter between the two has inspired artists, such as Tintoretto and Antonio Ciseri, and been explored in passion plays and more recently in films.

In the Lectionary

Luke's Passion Narrative (*Luke* 22:14-23:56), of which this is a part, is read on Palm Sunday in Year C.

Christ before Herod by Duccio di Buoninsegna (c. 1260-1318).

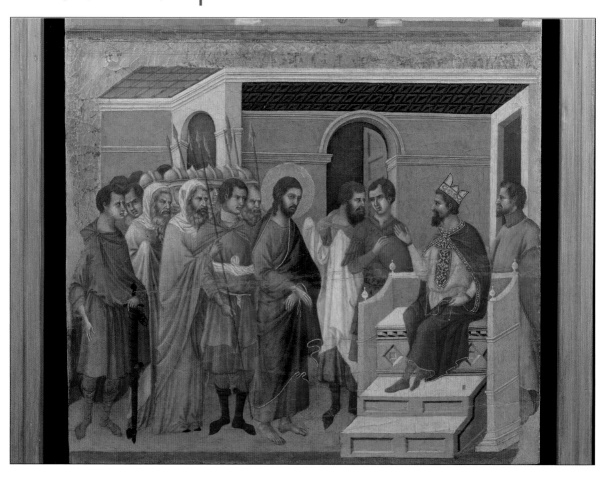

Live the Word of God

Listen again to the reading: Luke 23:1-25

What do you hear now?
Suggestions for reflection and prayer

Which characters of the passion story do you most readily identify with?

Reflect on the words of St Cyril of Jerusalem given in the margin.

St Cyril of Jerusalem writes:

'Herod and Pilate became friends that very day, whereas previously they had been at enmity with each other.' It was fitting that he, who was to restore peace between earth and heaven, should first put at peace the very men who condemned him, for the Lord himself was there present, 'who reconciles the hearts of the princes of the earth' (Job 12:24). (Catechetical Lectures 13.14).

Jesus was mocked by Herod and his soldiers.

❖ Pray for the courage to stand up for Christ in the face of mockery.

Pilate found Jesus innocent of the charges against him.

❖ Pray for those who are condemned unjustly, and all who are imprisoned for their beliefs.

Pilate released Barabbas in place of Jesus.

❖ Pray that Christ may release us from all that holds us prisoner.

Jesus is Crucified

Hear the Word of God

Read Luke 23:26-49

26 As they led him away, they seized a man, Simon of Cyrene, who was coming from the country, and they laid the cross on him, and made him carry it behind Jesus.

27 A great number of the people followed him, and among them were women who were beating their breasts and wailing for him. 28 But Jesus turned to them and said, 'Daughters of Jerusalem, do not weep for me, but weep for yourselves and for your children. 29 For the days are surely coming when they will say, 'Blessed are the barren, and the wombs that never bore, and the breasts that never nursed.' 30 Then they will begin to say to the mountains, 'Fall on us', and to the hills, 'Cover us.' 31 For if they do this when the wood is green, what will happen when it is dry?'

32 Two others also, who were criminals, were led away to be put to death with him. 33 When they came to the place that is called The Skull, they crucified Jesus there with the criminals, one on his right and one on his left. 34 Then Jesus said, 'Father, forgive them; for they do not know what they are doing.' And they cast lots to divide his clothing.

35 And the people stood by, watching; but the leaders scoffed at him, saying, 'He saved others; let him save himself if he is the Messiah of God, his chosen one!' 36 The soldiers also mocked him, coming up and offering him sour wine, 37 and saying, 'If you are the King of the Jews, save yourself!' 38 There was also an inscription over him, 'This is the King of the Jews.'

39 One of the criminals who were hanged there kept deriding him and saying, 'Are you not the Messiah? Save yourself and us!' 40 But the other rebuked him, saying, 'Do you not fear God, since you are under the same sentence of condemnation? 41 And we indeed have been condemned justly, for we are getting what we deserve for our deeds, but this man has done nothing wrong.' 42 Then he said, 'Jesus, remember me when you come into your kingdom.' 43 He replied, 'Truly I tell you, today you will be with me in Paradise.'

44 It was now about noon, and darkness came over the whole land until three in the afternoon, 45 while the sun's light failed; and the curtain of the temple was torn in two. 46 Then Jesus, crying with a loud voice, said, 'Father, into your hands I commend my spirit.' Having said this, he breathed his last.

47 When the centurion saw what had taken place, he praised God and said, 'Certainly this man was innocent.' 48 And when all the crowds who had gathered there for this spectacle saw what had taken place, they returned home, beating their breasts. 49 But all his acquaintances, including the women who had followed him from Galilee, stood at a distance, watching these things.

Opposite: I Thirst. The Vinegar Given to Jesus, illustration for 'The Life of Christ', c.1884-96 by Joseph Tissot, (1836-1902).

Understand the Word of God

This session will explore:

- ❖ Luke's special treatment of the crucifixion
- ❖ the characters in the passion story
- ❖ Luke's understanding of Christ's death
- ❖ the message for today

Setting in the Gospel

We now continue directly on from the story explored in the previous session. The murderer Barabbas has now been released, and Jesus faces crucifixion in his stead. At a deeper level, Luke points to the saving power of Christ's death: the innocent one dies in order that others may live.

As the next part of the story unfolds, Luke describes several characters, or sets of characters, who respond sympathetically to Jesus in his suffering. Three of them have already been encountered in Mark and Matthew: Simon of Cyrene, the centurion at the cross, and the women disciples from Galilee. To these Luke adds two others, who have fuelled the Christian imagination ever since: the weeping daughters of Jerusalem and the penitent thief.

What Kind of Text?

The passion narrative, as we have already seen, comprises a series of quite diverse types of text, bound together in a tight chronological framework. In this section, Luke includes a series of dialogues, through which Jesus continues to teach right up to his death.

Other details echo passages from the Old Testament. The dividing of Jesus' clothing and the offering of sour wine echoes Psalms 22:18 and 69:21. This is a sign that Jesus' death happens in fulfilment of God's will.

This passage breaks down into a series of shorter units: the journey to the cross (verses 26-31), the mocking of Jesus (verses 32-38), the dialogue with the two thieves (verses 39-43), and the death of Jesus and accompanying events (verses 44-49).

Psalm 22:18
They divide my clothes among themselves,
and for my clothing they cast lots.

Psalm 69:21
They gave me poison for food,
and for my thirst they gave me vinegar to drink.

Commentary: verse by verse reading

The Journey to the Cross

John 10:18 No one takes (my life) from me, but I lay it down of my own accord.

John 19:17 Carrying the cross by himself, he went out to what is called the Place of the Skull, which in Hebrew is called Golgotha.

Luke 9:23 If any want to become my followers, let them deny themselves and take up their cross daily and follow me.

Isaiah 62:11 The Lord has proclaimed to the end of the earth: Say to daughter Zion, 'See, your salvation comes; his reward is with him, and his recompense before him.'

Jeremiah 6:2 I have likened daughter Zion to the loveliest pasture.

Zechariah 9:9 Rejoice greatly, O daughter Zion! Shout aloud, O daughter Jerusalem! Lo, your king comes to you; triumphant and riding on a donkey, on a colt, the foal of a donkey.

v.26 Like Matthew and Mark, Luke refers to the episode of Simon of Cyrene. By contrast, John 10:18 and John 19:17 stress that Jesus carried his own cross without assistance. The name Simon (or Simeon) suggests that he is a Jew, from the North African city of Cyrene which had a large Jewish community.

According to Roman practice, Simon would have carried not the whole cross but the crossbeam (Latin *patibulum*). But Luke sees deeper significance in Simon's action. In carrying Jesus' cross, he becomes a model for all disciples, who are invited to take up their cross daily and follow Jesus (*Luke* 9:23).

vv.27-28 Just as Luke has described large crowds following Jesus on his journey to Jerusalem, now they accompany him to his journey's end. Among these, Luke singles out a group of women, calling them the 'daughters of Jerusalem'. This echoes the Old Testament description of Jerusalem as 'daughter Zion' (e.g. *Isaiah* 62:11; *Jeremiah* 6:2; *Zechariah* 9:9), pointing to the close relationship between the city and her inhabitants. The women whom Jesus encounters are beating their breasts, an action symbolising sorrow and repentance. Like so many others of their gender through Luke's gospel, and in sharp contrast to their leaders, they are able to see the truth about Jesus.

vv. 29-30 Jesus speaks to the women ominous words, which anticipate the destruction of Jerusalem by the Romans in AD 70, a past event known to Luke by the time he writes his gospel. But the overall note is one of Christ's sorrow and compassion.

We are reminded of Jesus' tears over the holy city at 19:41, and his prophecy of Jerusalem's fall at 21:23, which particularly singles out pregnant and nursing mothers. In verse 30 he envisages a time when the citizens of Jerusalem will repeat the ancient prophecy of Hosea: 'They shall say to the mountains, Cover us, and to the hills, Fall on us.' (*Hosea* 10:8) Nor are Jesus' words true only of first century Jerusalem: in every age it is women and their children who are particular victims of wars, sieges and other human tragedies.

v.31 Jesus' saying about the green and dry wood has puzzled many. In its context, it seems to address the violent reaction of Jerusalem and her leaders to the Prince of Peace. If they act thus now to the one who offers peace on earth (see 2:14), what hope can there be in the violent times ahead? Luke is probably thinking especially of the Jewish war against Rome, and the tragic events of AD 70. If so, then the metaphor of dry, kindling wood finds added poignancy, for the city was set ablaze by the Romans.

Luke 19:41 As he came near and saw the city, he wept over it.

Luke 21:23 Woe to those who are pregnant and to those who are nursing infants in those days!

Jesus and Simon of Cyrene by Titian (1477/89-1576).

The Mocking of the Messiah

v.32 All the gospels agree that Jesus was crucified along with two others. For Luke they are evil-doers, people who have broken the law. This fulfils the words from Isaiah quoted by Luke's Jesus at the Last Supper: 'And he was counted among the lawless' (22:37, quoting *Isaiah* 53:12).

v.33 Luke typically omits Aramaic names (here '*Golgotha*'), simply giving the Greek translation of the place of crucifixion, 'The Skull'. Most scholars assume it got its name from the skull-like shape of the hill, though later Christian tradition, understanding Jesus as the New Adam, locates it over Adam's grave. The traditional site of Golgotha is now within the Church of the Holy Sepulchre in the old city of Jerusalem.

Acts 7:60 describes the martyrdom of Stephen:

Then he knelt down and cried out in a loud voice, 'Lord, do not hold this sin against them.' When he had said this, he died.

v.34 The first part of this memorable verse is missing from some important early Greek manuscripts. Nevertheless, it is typically Lucan in its theme, and matches Stephen's prayer for his persecutors prior to his martyrdom at Acts 7:60. Some think it may have been removed by later scribes, who found its prayer of forgiveness for the Jewish leaders problematic.

If we count this verse as authentic, Luke records three sayings of Jesus from the cross, the other two being in verses 43 and 46. None of these sayings is mentioned by the other evangelists. They convey forgiveness towards others and trust towards the Father. Elsewhere in Luke, the experience of sins forgiven is an important aspect of the good news.

Luke 7:47 Therefore I tell you, her sins, which were many, have been forgiven; hence she has shown great love.
Luke 24:47 Repentance and forgiveness of sins is to be proclaimed in his name to all nations, beginning from Jerusalem.

Psalm 22:18
They divide my clothes among themselves,
and for my clothing they cast lots.

The action of the unnamed 'they', presumably the soldiers, underscores the depths of Christ's suffering. The last vestiges of his human possessions – his clothing – are taken away and divided by the casting of lots, which perhaps reflects a dice game played by the Roman army. For the early Christians, this is another sign that all is done to fulfil the scriptures, for it alludes to Psalm 22:18.

vv.35-37 Since Luke omitted the mock crowning of Jesus by the Roman soldiers, his account of Jesus' mockery at the cross appears all the more shocking. Here the derision of the soldiers, who call him 'King of the Jews', is more than matched by the leaders of his own people, who address him with the Jewish equivalent, 'the Messiah of God, his chosen one'. However, Luke has carefully distinguished the Jewish leaders from 'the people', who stand by watching, not joining in the mockery.

v.38 It was Roman practice to produce a notice or titulus, bearing the name of the person executed and the charge against them. All four gospels agree that the charge against Jesus, placed on the cross, included the words 'King of the Jews'. To Jewish ears, this declares Jesus to be the expected royal Messiah, the anointed king of David's line. To Roman sensibilities, it presents Jesus as a political agitator, a potential rival to Caesar Tiberius. But, as Luke has taught us, the kind of kingdom Jesus represents is very different from human notions of kingship.

Holy Sepulchre Basilica.

The Two Thieves

v.39 Although Matthew and Mark tell us of two criminals crucified with Jesus and taunting him, this beautiful scene is unique to Luke. As Simeon prophesied right at the beginning of the story (2:34), people would be divided over their attitude to Jesus. Right to the end, Jesus remains a sign that is rejected. Hence one of the criminals curses Jesus, in a mixture of mockery, which emulates that of the leaders and soldiers, and despair.

vv.40-41 The response of his fellow criminal, however, is utterly different. He speaks the truth, both about himself ('we indeed have been condemned justly') and about Jesus ('this man has done nothing wrong').

v.42 Unusually for the characters in Luke's Gospel, the penitent criminal addresses Christ as 'Jesus'. Perhaps the meaning of the name – 'the Lord saves' – is being evoked. The man sees what Jesus' kingdom is really like.

v.43 Jesus' reply is equally bold. 'Paradise' comes from a Persian word meaning a garden or enclosed space. It is used of the garden of Eden, and also of the abode of the righteous dead. Jesus assures the repentant criminal that he will have a place with him there. Perhaps Luke is hinting at Jesus as the new Adam, who reopens the gates of paradise.

There are a host of variant readings of this verse in the ancient manuscripts. Instead of 'when you come into your kingdom' other manuscripts read 'when you come in your kingdom' or 'in the day of your coming'.

St Ephrem the Syrian writes:

'There came to my ear
from the Scripture which had been read
a word that caused me joy
on the subject of the thief;
it gave comfort to my soul
amidst the multitude of its vices,
telling how he had compassion on the thief.
O may he bring me too
into that garden at the sound of whose name
I am overwhelmed by joy;
my mind bursts its reins
as it goes forth to contemplate him.'

(Hymn on Paradise 8.1).

The Death of Jesus

vv.44-45 The synoptic gospels agree that 'darkness' covered the land for three hours while Jesus hung on the cross, as Matthew 27:45 and Mark 15:33 show. But unlike Matthew and Mark, Luke does not see this darkness reflected in Jesus' own experience. His Jesus does not cry out 'My God, my God, why have you forsaken me?' Instead, Luke provides an explanation of why the darkness occurred ('the sun's light failed'), which might mean an eclipse of the sun. In this case, heaven is testifying to the extraordinary events taking place at Calvary. A natural solar eclipse would be impossible at the Passover full moon.

Luke also has the temple curtain tearing before Jesus dies, while in Matthew and Mark it happens afterwards. There were a number of curtains or veils in the Jerusalem Temple at the time of Jesus: most likely this was the veil which separated the Court of the Priests from the holy place, where incense was burned.

At the beginning of Luke's story, Zechariah the priest entered through that veil into the 'sanctuary' to burn incense (1:9). With the death of Jesus, the veil has been torn apart, allowing direct access to God's presence to all God's people, even those who are not priests.

v.46 Luke's Jesus utters dying words of serenity and trust, in keeping with Luke's overall portrayal of Jesus. This would appeal to non-Jewish, particularly Greek, audiences. Nevertheless, his words are words from the Jewish Scriptures, in this case Psalm 31:6. It is Israel's God, not any Greek or Roman deity, in whom he puts his hope.

v.47 The centurion at the cross would be a Roman soldier, and therefore presumably a Gentile. He is a reminder that Luke's good news is addressed to the non-Jewish world as well as the people of Israel.

Psalm 31:4-6
You are indeed my rock and my fortress;
for your name's sake lead me and guide me;
take me out of the net that is hidden for me,
for you are my refuge.
Into your hand I commit my spirit;
you have redeemed me, O Lord, faithful God.

Acts 3:14-15

Peter said: 'But you rejected the Holy and Righteous One and asked to have a murderer given to you, and you killed the Author of life, whom God raised from the dead. To this we are witnesses.'

1 John 2:1 If anyone does sin, we have an advocate with the Father, Jesus Christ the righteous.

The centurion's response differs here from the version in Matthew and Mark: he declares Jesus 'innocent' (Greek *dikaios*). From the centurion's perspective, this is probably a recognition that Jesus was unjustly executed. But the word can also mean 'righteous', and Christian readers are probably to understand this deeper sense. Within the early church, one of the titles used of Christ was the 'Righteous One'.

v.48 Throughout the passion story, Luke has been careful to distinguish between the crowds and the authorities in their response to Jesus. Now, at the end of a story in which the dying Jesus has offered forgiveness to the penitent, the crowds show signs of repentance. As they return from witnessing Jesus' death, Luke tells us that they were 'beating their breasts', like the women of Jerusalem at verse 27.

v.49 Finally, Luke describes Jesus' acquaintances, emphasising the place of the women who had followed him from Galilee. We have already met this faithful group of female disciples at 8:2-3. Luke stresses the importance of witnesses, those who have seen and understood, and who are able to testify to the truth of the good news.

As we prepare for their witness to the resurrection at the empty tomb, these women are introduced again, standing 'watching these things'. They remind us of Mary, the first disciple, who 'treasured all these words and pondered them in her heart' (2:19).

Opposite: Christ Between the Two Thieves, 1620 by Peter Rubens, (1577-1640).

The Word Lives on

Again, Luke's story is paralleled in the other gospels, particularly Matthew and Mark. Some of the most memorable features, however, are Luke's alone: the women of Jerusalem, the prayer for forgiveness and the penitent thief.

Later tradition gave the penitent thief a name (Dismas), and medieval artists often depicted him alongside Christ in their portrayals of the descent into hell. In popular devotion, the daughters of Jerusalem are especially recalled in the eighth Station of the Cross.

In the Lectionary

Luke's Passion Narrative (*Luke* 22:14-23:56), of which this is a part, is read on Palm Sunday in Year C. Part of Luke's crucifixion scene (*Luke* 23:35-43) is also set for the Solemnity of Christ the King in Year C. If we want to understand Christ's kingship, Calvary is a good place to start.

The Daughters of Jerusalem, 1951 by Stanley Spencer(1891-1959).

Live the Word of God

Listen again to the reading: Luke 23:26-49

What do you hear now?
Suggestions for reflection and prayer

Which features of Luke's story strike you most forcefully?

Meditate upon the words of Pope John Paul II given in the margin.

Simon of Cyrene was compelled to carry Jesus' cross.
❖ Pray for the grace to recognise Christ in those who suffer, and to shoulder their burdens.

The daughters of Jerusalem wept for Jesus.
❖ Pray for the peace of Jerusalem, and its divided children.

The penitent criminal spoke the truth about himself, and asked to be remembered in Jesus' kingdom.
❖ Pray for the courage to acknowledge the truth about ourselves, and the joy of accepting Christ's forgiveness.

Each time we approach Christ being scourged or Christ on Calvary there is a real possibility that something will be stirred in us and we shall change.

(John Paul II, The Way to Christ)

Meeting the Risen Lord

Hear the Word of God

Read Luke 24:36-53

³⁶ While they were talking about this, Jesus himself stood among them and said to them, 'Peace be with you.' ³⁷ They were startled and terrified, and thought that they were seeing a ghost.

³⁸ He said to them, 'Why are you frightened, and why do doubts arise in your hearts? ³⁹ Look at my hands and my feet; see that it is I myself. Touch me and see; for a ghost does not have flesh and bones as you see that I have.' ⁴⁰ And when he had said this, he showed them his hands and his feet.

⁴¹ While in their joy they were disbelieving and still wondering, he said to them, 'Have you anything here to eat?' ⁴² They gave him a piece of broiled fish, ⁴³ and he took it and ate in their presence.

⁴⁴ Then he said to them, 'These are my words that I spoke to you while I was still with you-- that everything written about me in the law of Moses, the prophets, and the psalms must be fulfilled.'

⁴⁵ Then he opened their minds to understand the scriptures, ⁴⁶ and he said to them, 'Thus it is written, that the Messiah is to suffer and to rise from the dead on the third day, ⁴⁷ and that repentance and forgiveness of sins is to be proclaimed in his name to all nations, beginning from Jerusalem. ⁴⁸ You are witnesses of these things. ⁴⁹ And see, I am sending upon you what my Father promised; so stay here in the city until you have been clothed with power from on high.'

⁵⁰ Then he led them out as far as Bethany, and, lifting up his hands, he blessed them. ⁵¹ While he was blessing them, he withdrew from them and was carried up into heaven. ⁵² And they worshipped him, and returned to Jerusalem with great joy; ⁵³ and they were continually in the temple blessing God.

Opposite: Resurrection, Raffaellino del Garbo, (c.1466-1524).

Understand the Word of God

This session will explore:

- ❖ the gospel resurrection stories
- ❖ the place of this story in Luke's narrative
- ❖ Luke's understanding of the resurrection
- ❖ the message for today

Setting in the Gospel

For Christians, the story of Jesus does not end with his death. Hence all four gospels describe how, on the third day after his crucifixion, women followers find his tomb empty. Luke's version (*Luke* 24:1-12) concludes in some manuscripts with Peter going to the tomb, providing male verification of the testimony of inadmissible (female) witnesses.

Nor is even this the end: Luke, like Matthew and John, and the longer ending of Mark in Mark 16:9-20, continues with stories in which the risen Lord appears to his disciples. Unique to him is the beautiful dramatic account of the road to Emmaus, at the end of which two disciples recognise Jesus in the breaking of the bread (*Luke* 24:13-35). The passage for study, which concludes the gospel and provides a bridge to the Acts of the Apostles, follows immediately after the Emmaus episode.

What Kind of Text?

The resurrection appearance stories are like complex tapestries, weaving together memories of what happened to the disciples on the first Easter with the Church's ongoing experience of the risen Lord, particularly in the liturgy. They attempt to describe the unknown –the resurrection of Jesus – in the language of what we know. So they are based on the real experiences of those first disciples in Jerusalem, narrated in Luke 24 and John 20, and in Galilee, narrated in Matthew 28 and John 21.

But they also aim to teach us how we can encounter the risen Lord today in as real a way as they did. This passage is one complete story, which presupposes the previous story of Emmaus. For ease of study, it can be subdivided into three: the appearance in Jerusalem (verses 36-43); Jesus explains the scriptures (verses 44-49); the ascension from Bethany (verses 50-53).

The Supper at Emmaus by Michelangelo Caravaggio

Commentary: verse by verse reading

The Appearance in Jerusalem

1 Corinthians 15:3-5:

For I handed on to you as of first importance what I in turn had received: that Christ died for our sins in accordance with the scriptures, and that he was buried, and that he was raised on the third day in accordance with the scriptures, and that he appeared to Cephas, then to the twelve.

v.36 This episode takes place on the same evening as the supper at Emmaus, Easter Day. Earliest Christian tradition tells us that Christ appeared 'to the Twelve' after he was raised (1 *Corinthians* 15:5). This is important, because the Twelve have been commissioned to continue Christ's own ministry. Luke is rather more precise. Jesus appears to the 'eleven', for Judas Iscariot is no longer with them, and 'their companions' gathered in Jerusalem (verse 33).

Jesus' greeting, 'Peace be with you', is the typical Jewish greeting 'Shalom'. This has the wider sense of well-being, peace with God and our brothers and sisters. The resurrection breaks down any barriers to true peace and reconciliation.

v.37 The terrified reaction of the disciples may initially surprise us. Luke is wanting to teach us that the risen Jesus is both the same Jesus and yet different, transformed. Hence the disciples mistake him for a disembodied spirit or ghost.

vv.38-40 But Luke is also keen to make clear that this is no disembodied 'spirit'. The risen Christ has flesh and bones. Some Greeks believed that the essential person was the 'soul', temporarily imprisoned in a body. For the Semitic world, however, to be fully human is to be embodied. It is through our bodies that we relate to one another. Hence Luke stresses the tangible, bodily nature of Christ's risen life. The disciples, like Thomas at John 20:26-29, are invited to touch and see.

Matthew 28:17 When they saw him they worshipped him; but some doubted.

Luke 24:30 When he was at table with them, he took bread, blessed and broke it, and gave it to them.

John 21:13 Jesus came and took the bread and gave it to them, and did the same with the fish.

vv.41-43 Even when Jesus has identified himself, Luke describes a mixed reaction from the disciples. Their joy is mixed with disbelief and wondering, as in Matthew 28:17. This is dispelled by Jesus eating a piece of fish, which confirms that he is no mere spirit. Luke alone among the gospels tells us that the risen Lord ate something. Elsewhere it is he who feeds others, in Luke 24:30 and John 21:13, as he continues to feed us in the Eucharist.

Explaining the Scriptures

v.44 One of Luke's aims has been to show the fulfilment of God's promises to the people of Israel in the life, death and resurrection of Jesus. God is a God who can be trusted. What happened to Jesus was not mere chance, but part of God's plan. Luke provides an early example here of the Jewish threefold division of the Old Testament: the Law (the Pentateuch or five 'books of Moses'), the Prophets and the Writings (he refers specifically to 'the psalms').

Even prior to his crucifixion, Luke's Jesus foretold that what would happen to him is in accordance with the Old Testament scriptures.

v.45 At Emmaus, the eyes of the two disciples' were opened, enabling them to recognise Jesus (24:31). Here too Jesus opens the disciples minds to understand the scriptures.

v.46 It is difficult to identify the specific Old Testament passages which Luke has in mind. The Old Testament does not unambiguously prophesy a suffering and rising Messiah. However, in the light of Jesus, the early Christians came to read ancient scriptures in a new way. They made sense of Christ's death through psalms which speak of innocent suffering (e.g. *Psalms* 22 and 69), or Isaiah's songs of a mysterious Suffering Servant (e.g. *Isaiah* 53). They understood prophecies of the restoration of God's people (e.g. *Hosea* 6:2) as referring to Christ's resurrection.

v.47 A typical element of the resurrection appearance stories is a commission. The risen Lord sends out his disciples to continue his mission. The language of the commission here is typical of Luke. The good news is about a God who forgives sins, and who invites human beings to 'repent', to change their minds. Moreover, it is good news for all the nations of the world, a universal theme present from the beginning of Luke's gospel.

Luke 18:31 reads:

Then he took the twelve aside and said to them, 'See, we are going up to Jerusalem, and everything that is written about the Son of Man by the prophets will be accomplished.'

Isaiah 53:4-5

Surely he has borne our infirmities and carried our diseases;
yet we accounted him stricken, struck down by God, and afflicted.
But he was wounded for our transgressions,
crushed for our iniquities;
upon him was the punishment that made us whole,
And by his bruises we are healed.

Hosea 6:2

After two days he will revive us;
on the third day he will raise us up, that we may live before him.

Jerusalem is the starting-point, for God remains faithful to his ancient people, the Jews. All Luke's resurrection stories take place in or around Jerusalem. In the Acts of the Apostles, the gospel will spread out from Jerusalem. Even Paul, the apostle to the Gentiles, will regularly return to Jerusalem as the holy city and mother-church (*Acts* 15:2; 18:22 and 21:17).

v.48 Witness is an important concept in Luke-Acts. The Church's preaching is grounded in the testimony of reliable witnesses, who can provide assurance of its truth (*Luke* 1:1-4). Indeed, for Luke, being a witness to the resurrection is one of the criteria for being an apostle, as is demonstrated when the apostles choose someone to replace Judas (*Acts* 1:21-22).

v.49 The 'power from on high' for which the disciples must wait is the gift of the Holy Spirit. This promise will be fulfilled in the story of Pentecost in Acts 2. But it is not confined to the first Pentecost. As Acts makes clear, the Holy Spirit continues to empower the Church through fresh outpourings (e.g. *Acts* 4:31 and 10:44).

The Departure from Bethany

v.50 Bethany (meaning 'house of figs') is a village on the Mount of Olives, about three miles east of Jerusalem. It is from Bethany and nearby Bethphage that Jesus began his entry into Jerusalem on a colt (*Luke* 19:29). According to John, Bethany was the village of Lazarus, Mary and Martha (*John* 11:1).

Luke portrays Jesus as a priest, who raises his hands in blessing over the worshipping disciples. We are reminded of Aaron blessing the Israelites at Leviticus 9:22 or ben-Sira's description of the High Priest Simon (*Sirach* 50:20-21). In the New Testament, the Letter to the Hebrews also thinks of Jesus as a high priest, who enters into the heavenly sanctuary at his ascension.

Leviticus 9:22

Aaron lifted his hands towards the people and blessed them.

Sirach (Ecclesiasticus) 50:20-21

Then Simon came down and raised his hands over the whole congregation of Israelites,
to pronounce the blessing of the Lord with his lips,
and to glory in his name;
and they bowed down in worship a second time,
to receive the blessing from the Most High.

v.51 The ending of Luke's gospel prepares us for the beginning of Acts. Jesus must withdraw in order that the disciples can receive the Spirit and fulfil their mission. The specific reference to the ascension ('and was carried up into heaven') is missing in some ancient manuscripts. However, it is likely to be original. Later scribes may have omitted these words because they seem to contradict Acts 1:1-11. According to Acts, Jesus appeared for forty days prior to his ascension, whereas this verse implies that the ascension occurred on Easter Day.

The ascension is important both for Christ and for us. For Christ, it means that he enters 'into his glory' (24:26). But the ascension also means that our human nature now shares God's life. In the ascension, it is a human body, one of us, who now shares God's throne.

St Athanasius wrote:

He became human that we might become divine.

(On the Incarnation 54)

vv.52-53 The priestly theme continues in the response of the disciples. They worship the ascending Lord, then return to Jerusalem to continue that worship in the temple. Thus Luke's Gospel ends where it began, in the temple in Jerusalem.

Opposite: The Ascensionby Andrea Della Robbia, (1435-1525/28).

The Word Lives on

Among the gospels, Luke's appearance to the Eleven is most closely paralleled in John 20. The invitation here to look at and touch Jesus' hands and feet echoes John's story of Thomas (*John* 20:19-21). The reference to fish parallels another Easter story in John, set by the Sea of Galilee (*John* 21:9-14). The ascension of Jesus is also described in the longer ending to Mark (*Mark* 16:19).

In the Lectionary

From the Preface for the Mass of the Solemnity of the Ascension:

Christ is the beginning, the head of the Church;

where he has gone, we hope to follow.

Part of this passage (*Luke* 24:35-48) is the Gospel for the Third Sunday of Easter in Year B. The same passage is in the Weekday Lectionary for Thursday in the Octave of Easter. The final section (*Luke* 24:46-53) is read, appropriately, on the Ascension of the Lord in Year C.

The Ascension by Thomas Kolozsvari, (15th century).

Live the Word of God

Listen again to the reading: Luke 24:36-53

What do you hear now?

Suggestions for reflection and prayer

What has struck you most in your reading of the Gospel of Luke?

Meditate on the words about the ascension by Pope St Leo the Great given in the margin.

The risen Lord stood among his disciples and said 'Peace be with you.'

❖ Pray for the peace of the risen Christ in the lives of all who long for peace.

Jesus opened the disciples' minds to understand the scriptures.

❖ Pray for a greater love of scripture, and a desire to study it more deeply.

Christ promised his Church the 'power from on high'.

❖ Pray for a deeper openness to the work of the Holy Spirit in our lives.

St Leo the Great writes:

The ascension of Christ is our elevation. Hope for the body is also invited where the glory of the Head preceded us. Let us exult, dearly beloved, with worthy joy and be glad with a holy thanksgiving. Today we not only are established as possessors of paradise, but we have even penetrated the heights of the heavens in Christ.

(Sermon 73)

Picture Credits

Cover   St Luke, c700, British Library, London. ©Photo Scala Florence/HIP.

P.9   ©HellenicArt.com

P.11   The Annunciation, c.1438-45, Angelico, Fra (Guido di Pietro) (c.1387-1455) / Museo di San Marco dell'Angelico, Florence, Italy / The Bridgeman Art Library.

P.12   The Visitation, Bruyn, Bartholomaeus (1493-1555) / Rafael Valls Gallery, London, UK / The Bridgeman Art Library.

P.15   ©Bibleplaces.com

P.16   The Visitation. ©JesusMafa.com

P.17   The Visitation, Weyden, Rogier van der (1399-1464) / Galleria Sabauda, Turin, Italy / The Bridgeman Art Library.

P.18   La visitation : Marie rend visite a Elisabeth. 16th cent , School of Troyes, St.-Jean-au-Marche, Troyes, France. © White Images/Scala, Florence.

P.20   The Nativity, c.1305, Giotto di Bondone (c.1266-1337) / Scrovegni (Arena) Chapel, Padua, Italy / The Bridgeman Art Library.

P.23   Statue of Caesar at the Vatican in Rome. ©Photos.com

P.24   Church of the Nativity, Bethlehem. ©Stock.Xchng

P.25   The New Born Child, late 1640s, Georges de la Tour, (1593-1652) / Musee des Beaux-Arts, Rennes, France / Giraudon / The Bridgeman Art Library

P.27   The Annunciation to the Shepherds, Cuyp, Gerritsz Benjamin. (1612-52) / Hermitage, St. Petersburg, Russia / The Bridgeman Art Library

P.29   The Adoration of the Shepherds by Andrea Mantegna, 1450. ©Photos.com

P.30   Statue of the Blessed Virgin Mary and Christ, ©Michael Ziegler, www.mzig.com

P.32   Jesus teaching in the Synagogue, c. 1897 (from 'Life of Our Saviour Jesus Christ' by J.J. Tissot, London, c. 1897). ©Photo Ann Ronan/HIP/Scala, Florence

P.36   Our Saviour Subject to his Parents at Nazareth, 1860, John Rogers Herbert, (1810-90) / Private Collection / Photo © Christie's Images / The Bridgeman Art Library

P.37   Israel - Israel Museum - Isaiah Scroll of the Dead Sea Scrolls. ©Jim Hollander/epa/Corbis

P.38   Interior of the Ancient Synagogue at Nazareth / Private Collection / Roger-Viollet, Paris / The Bridgeman Art Library

P.39   Basilica of the Annunciation Nazareth. ©Photos.com

P.41   Print Depicting Elijah Carried to Heaven in a Fiery Chariot While Watched by Elisha. © Historical Picture Archive/CORBIS

P.92   The Rich Man and Lazarus. ©JesusMafa.com

P.95   Hebew Bible. ©Stock.Xchng

P.96   The Death of Lazarus and the Rich Man, from a capital in the nave, c.1150 (photo), French School, (12th century) / La Madeleine, Vezelay, France / Lauros / Giraudon / The Bridgeman Art Library

P.98   Jesus Christ entering Jerusalem. From 'The Benedictional of St Aethelwold', c. 971-c. 984. Godeman (d. 984), British Library, London, Great Britain. ©Photo Scala Florence/HIP

P.101   W.912 fol.106v Christ Enters Jerusalem, Ethiopian School, (18th century) / The Trustees of the Chester Beatty Library, Dublin / The Bridgeman Art Library

P.103   ©Stock.Xchng

P.104   The Triumphant Entry into Jerusalem. ©JesusMafa.com

P.107   Jerusalem. ©Photos.com

P.108   Palm Sunday celebrations in Israel. ©Photos.com

P.110   Ms Fr 71 fol.17 Jesus before Pilate, from The Hours of the Cross and the Holy Spirit, from the 'Heures d'Etienne Chevalier', c.1445, Fouquet, Jean (c.1420-80) / Musee Conde, Chantilly, France / Lauros / Giraudon / The Bridgeman Art Library

P.113   Jesus before Pilate, Church of Sant' Apollinare Nuovo, Ravenna, Italy. © Photo Scala, Florence - courtesy of the Ministero Beni e Att. Culturali

P.115   Christ Before Pilate, c.1530, Mazzolino, Lodovico (c.1479-c.1528) / Fitzwilliam Museum, University of Cambridge, UK / The Bridgeman Art Library

P.119   Christ before Pilate, Pietro Lorenzetti, (1280-c. 1348), Pinacoteca, Vatican, Vatican City. ©Photo Scala, Florence

P.120   Maesta, back: Christ before Herod, Duccio di Buoninsegna (c. 1260-1318). Museo dell'Opera Metropolitana, Siena, Italy. ©Photo Opera Metropolitana Siena/Scala, Florence

P.122   I Thirst. The Vinegar Given to Jesus, illustration for 'The Life of Christ', c.1884-96,James Jacques Joseph Tissot, (1836-1902) / Brooklyn Museum of Art, New York, USA / The Bridgeman Art Library

P.125   ©Photos.com

P.127   Jesus and Simon of Cyrene , Titian (1477/89-1576) Prado, Madrid, Spain. ©Photo Scala, Florence.

P.129   Holy Sepulchre Basilica. ©BiblePlaces.com

P.133   Christ Between the Two Thieves, 1620, Peter Paul Rubens, (1577-1640) / Koninklijk Museum voor Schone Kunsten, Antwerp, Belgium / Giraudon / The Bridgeman Art Library

P.134   The Daughters of Jerusalem, 1951, Stanley Spencer, (1891-1959) / Private Collection / © DACS / Susannah Pollen Ltd / The Bridgeman Art Library

P.136   Resurrection, Garbo, Raffaellino del (c.1466-1524) / Galleria dell' Accademia, Florence, Italy / The Bridgeman Art Library

P.139   The Supper at Emmaus, 1601 Michelangelo Caravaggio, Merisi da (1571-1610) / National Gallery, London, UK / The Bridgeman Art Library

P.142   The Ascension, Andrea Della Robbia, (1435-1525/28) / Museo Nazionale del Bargello, Florence, Italy / The Bridgeman Art Library

P.144   The Ascension, Thomas Kolozsvari, Thomas (15th century) / Christian Museum, Esztergom, Hungary / The Bridgeman Art Library

Notes

Notes